FINDING YOUR BIBLE

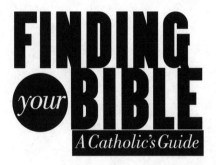

FINDING your BIBLE
A Catholic's Guide

TIMOTHY SCHEHR

ST. ANTHONY MESSENGER PRESS

Cincinnati, Ohio

Scripture citations are taken from *New Revised Standard Version Bible,* copyright
©1989 by the Division of Christian Education of the National Council of the
Churches of Christ in the U.S.A., and used by permission. All rights reserved.

Cover and book design by Mark Sullivan

Library of Congress Cataloging-in-Publication Data

Schehr, Timothy.
  Finding your Bible : a Catholic's guide / Timothy Schehr.
      p. cm.
Includes bibliographical references.
  ISBN 0-86716-545-6 (alk. paper)
  1. Bible—Introductions. 2. Catholic Church—Doctrines. I. Title.

  BS475.3.S34 2004
  220.6'1'024282—dc22

                                             2003025700

ISBN 0–86716–545–6

Copyright ©2004, Timothy Schehr
All rights reserved.

Published by St. Anthony Messenger Press
www.AmericanCatholic.org
Printed in the U.S.A.

CONTENTS

INTRODUCTION

This book is a collection of my favorite insights regarding the Bible. If you are not very familiar with the Bible, this book may get you interested in reading the Bible. If you already do read the Bible, this book may help you get more out of what you read. You might think of it as adding color to your reading.

For many, the Bible can be intimidating at first look. For one thing, it is a long book. There are many chapters between its covers. The Bible can be physically large as well. There is at least one Bible that weighs nearly seventy-five pounds. In the time of Henry VIII an English Bible published in 1539 was so big it was called, quite appropriately, The Great Bible. When I was growing up, our Bible at home didn't weigh quite that much but it was still pretty hefty to carry around.

Once you get over the sheer size of the book, you still have to confront the appearance of its inner pages. The standard two-column presentation has been with us since the days when Bibles were produced by hand. Page after page of this format can dampen the resolve of the best of us to launch into a prolonged reading.

Another reason why people might be intimidated by the Bible is the fact that there is so much scholarship associated with it. Commentaries, dictionaries and journals on the Bible abound. An ordinary person might think he or she could not possibly be educated enough to open the book and actually be qualified to read it.

But don't let these reasons or any other put you off. Reading the Bible is full of life and blessings. You simply need to take the time to become familiar with it. And that is precisely the purpose of this book.

In addition to some helpful hints scattered throughout the book, each chapter ends with a "For Reflection" section. These questions are designed especially for groups who are using this book as an aid to Scripture study, but you can easilty adapt them for your personal use.

CHAPTER ONE: THE BOOK AND THE FINE PRINT

The Bible is a great spiritual treasury. Its message has enriched more than a hundred generations reaching all way back to the centuries before the birth of Jesus. But unless you are one of those fortunate few who can read the Bible in its original languages, you need a find a good translation to gain access to its riches. Fortunately there are many translations available in English. This chapter will help you discover a translation of the Bible that you find comfortable and accessible.

Let's imagine you are walking into a bookstore for the first time to buy a Bible. What will you see? Probably (and this, of course, depends on the specialty of the store you enter) you will find at the very least several shelves full of Bibles of many different colors and sizes. Some Bibles will be boxed; some will not. Some will have leather or leather-like covers; some will come in paperback. It can all be pretty intimidating at first glance. How do you begin sorting through all the options?

CHOOSING A TRANSLATION

Take your time and step back. You will notice that for the most part there are only a handful of different translations represented on the shelves in front of you. One of the titles you will certainly see is the

Revised Standard Version. This one has been around for a long time. This is a revision of the "standard version," which is the King James translation going all the way back to 1611. Some publishers call the King James version the "authorized version." Another Bible you will find on the shelf is a relatively recent arrival, the New International Version. You may also see the Today's English Version, more popularly known as the Good News Bible. Another recent addition to the Bible shelf is the New Living Translation (NLT). Some stores may also carry the New English Bible and the recent Contemporary English Version (especially good for young readers). Catholic readers will be familiar with the Jerusalem Bible and the New American Bible (NAB). This last one should sound familiar to Catholics since it is the one most parishes use for the Sunday readings.

†

You might think picture Bibles are something new. But already in the time of Saint Francis of Assisi picture books based on the Bible were very popular. A biblical scene was often paired with another scene from everyday life. By comparing the two the reader discovered a rich lesson in moral virtue.

This is the list of translations you are most likely to see on a bookstore shelf. If you see others, just ask your friendly bookseller to give you some assistance.

Now, beyond all of these translations, you will notice that each translation comes in several different packages, or editions. You will find deluxe editions (the kind you might consider for wedding or anniversary gifts), pocket-sized editions, coffee-table editions (those really big ones) and everyday-use editions. Don't worry about which edition to choose just yet. Your first task is to find a translation with which you are comfortable.

Use your favorite Bible passage as a way of testing out each translation. Pick a translation and read your favorite passage aloud to yourself (but not so loudly as to distract the person next to you who may be doing exactly the same thing). Listen to the way it sounds. Do you like it? Or is there something missing for you? Pick up a different translation and do the same thing. Keep going until you have gone through all the translations you care to consider.

A wonderful test-passage is Psalm 23. Here is the beginning of the psalm in two translations:

The New Living Translation:
> The Lord is my shepherd;
> I have everything I need.
> He lets me rest in green meadows;
> he leads me beside peaceful streams.

The New American Bible:
> The Lord is my shepherd;
> there is nothing I lack.
> In green pastures you let
> me graze;
> to safe waters you
> lead me;

†

Early printed Bibles featured lots of notes in the margins. In time these marginal notes became so controversial that the translators of the King James Bible were forbidden to include any, except those necessary to explain the meaning of a word

I like the natural sound of the first translation. The verse "I have every-thing I need" appeals to me because it is such a strong assertion of faith in God, the sort of ideal faith I am con-stantly struggling for in my own life. I also like the quiet and peacefulness of the second verse. Green meadows and peaceful streams are just what I need on a hectic day. Even if I can't get to such places on a given day, this verse at least lets me think about them.

The language of the NAB is a little more formal. "There is nothing I lack" is not the way I speak normally. But then again, maybe it's a good thing to make the Bible sound a little less like ordinary speech since the Bible is, after all, the word of God. The second verse in the NAB does not present as restful a scene as the one in the NLT. Instead of resting, I'm grazing in the green grass. And the phrase "safe waters" is a little puzzling. What makes them safe? Are they less deep than other waters? Are they free from pollution? Are they free of sharks or pirates? On the other hand, the more I read over the NAB translation of this psalm, the more I find attractive about it. I hear the repetition in the words "lack," "let" and "lead." This gives the psalm a greater poetic quality.

Choosing between these two translations is not easy. There are things to recommend them both. Honestly, I would probably buy both of them. But at least I have given you an idea of the sort of thoughts that might go through your mind as you test out different translations.

You may discover that you have difficulty deciding on one translation. If you can afford it, it might be good to have more than one translation. It is like having more than one recording of a favorite piece of music. You have choices depending on your mood.

THE BOOKS OF THE BIBLE

One important thing to keep in mind when choosing a Bible is that some Bibles include more books than others. To explain this, a very quick and simplified history review may be of help.

In its early years the church knew the entire Bible in the Greek language. This should not be too surprising since the Gospels and Paul's letters were written in Greek. Ordinary church members were probably not even aware that some books in their Old Testament were not included in the Bible heard and read by the Jews.

But informed people, like Saint Jerome for example, knew that some books of the Greek Old Testament could not be found in the Hebrew Bible. Saint Jerome had a personal preference for those books that were in Hebrew. But his preference had no impact on the actual appearance of the Bible. When the books of the Bible were bound in a single volume—and we have some of these from as far back as the fourth century—the books of the Old Testament appeared as a unit with no visual separation of those in the Hebrew Bible from those that were not. This was the tradition for centuries.

In the early sixteenth century reformers in the church returned with renewed interest to the differences between the Greek Bible and the Hebrew Bible. And they took those differences a step further. For the first time the Old Testament books in the Hebrew Bible were visually separated from those that were not. A complete Bible printed in 1534 was among the first to include a new and separate section entitled "The Apocrypha." Into this new section were gathered all the books not in the Hebrew Bible. This new section was placed after the Old Testament prophets and before the New Testament. Readers now saw a Bible with three main parts instead of the traditional two. Within a century this new and separate portion of apocrypha was being dropped altogether from some printed editions of the Bible.

The Roman Catholic Church retained the Bible in its traditional form. But for the first time church leaders found it necessary to list in a formal way the books traditionally belonging to the Bible so there would be no confusion about it for Catholics. And so in 1546 the Council of Trent listed the books in a formal decree. Unlike the reformers at that time, the council made no distinction among the books of the Old Testament with regard to origin, stating simply that it accepted as the word of God all the books of the Old and the New Testament.

So when you choose your Bible you must make certain you get what you want. If you are a Roman Catholic, you will definitely want to have a Bible that includes all the books traditionally belonging to the Old Testament. A Bible produced by Catholics will, of course, include them. For English speakers that means the New American Bible or the Jerusalem Bible. Many Bibles generated by other denominations also include them though they separate them from the rest of the Old Testament and print them under the heading Apocrypha.

A Catholic edition of the Revised Standard Version, published originally in 1966 and now available from Ignatius Press, includes all the Old Testament books in their traditional places. The same is true of a Catholic edition of the New Revised Standard Version, published in 1999.

Somebody came up with this clever phrase for remembering the Old Testament books that do not appear in the Hebrew Bible: "J. T. Web and the two McCabes." When we unpack the phrase we get Judith, Tobit, Wisdom, Ecclesiasticus, Baruch, and I and II Maccabees. This is helpful as far as it goes. But just remember, in addition to these seven books there are also additions to Esther and Daniel.

CHOOSE AN EDITION THAT'S RIGHT FOR YOU

Once you find a translation you like, the next step is to select an edition that will meet your needs. First, choose the size and style you like best. Then you can begin to consider the subtle differences in content. Some Bibles offer a fairly simple rendition of the text. Others can be very elaborate. Even the simplest edition will probably have some notes at the bottom of each page. Most of the time such notes are there to clarify a word or passage, or to inform you of alternative readings. Take, for example, a simple edition of the Revised Standard Version. On the bottom of the first page there is a note explaining that another way to translate the first line of Genesis is "When God began to create…" instead of the standard "In the beginning God created…" Another footnote on the same page suggests that it might be interesting to compare the first line of John's Gospel with the first line of Genesis.

Of course, some Bibles can include a lot more than a few simple notes. Some editions include an introduction to each book of the Bible, lists of words and their explanations and even colorful maps. In recent years, study Bibles have become popular. They typically include many pages explaining each book of the Bible (historical background, outline, principal themes and so on) so that you can really get a grasp on what you are reading. Some editions include a running commentary to help you apply the text to your life or help you meditate on its meaning. This is typical of Bibles that have words like "meditation" or "life application" on their covers. Choose the edition that you find most inviting.

READING THE FINE PRINT

What about all those tiny notes? Are they worth reading? Or are they full of jargon so technical no ordinary person could understand it? They are definitely worth reading. And, with some time and practice, you will master all those numbers and abbreviations that look like gibberish at first glance.

The fine print in most Bibles offers two things that are very useful for the Bible reader: footnotes and cross-references.

Footnotes cover many interesting points. Very often they offer explanations of details within the main text: the meaning of a name, for example, or a word-play in the original language. Sometimes they clarify a passage that might be obscure. In almost every case, your appreciation of the text will be enriched by taking the time to read the notes.

The second feature offered by the fine print is, I think, even more interesting: cross-references. These are lists of other passages in the Bible that connect in some way with the passage you are actually reading. At first glance they are a little daunting: abbreviated titles of biblical books followed by chapter and verse. But if you take the time to look up these cross-references, you may discover some real gems.

Let's take a closer look at the fine print. Each Bible handles the fine print a little differently. To be most helpful, here we will consider each of the translations American Catholic readers are most likely to use.

THE NEW AMERICAN BIBLE

If you glance at the bottom of a page of biblical text, you will normally see the two sets of notes divided from each other by a blank space.

The first set is in sentence or paragraph form preceded by a reference to the chapter and verse the note comments on. For example, on the first page of Genesis you will see a note at the bottom that begins: "1,1—2,4a: This section introduces..." This note comments about the entire portion of Genesis starting at chapter one, verse one and concluding at chapter two, verse 4a. (The *a* means the first part of the verse. Sometimes verses span ideas or, as in this case, even paragraphs.) It explains that these verses present God as making order out of chaos. The note also says this section introduces the entire Book of Genesis, suggesting to me that maybe a good way to think about God as we read this book is to think of God as making sense out of the confusion people introduce in the world.

The next paragraph begins: "1,2: The abyss..." This note comments on the meaning of this fascinating word found in Genesis 1:2. At first reading we might associate the word *abyss* with some deep dark hole in the ground. But actually, as the note explains, it refers to the great expanse of water the ancients believed surrounded this world.

As you can see, there is a wealth of information in such notes. Your reading of the Bible will be enriched by taking the time to read them. Wherever you see an asterisk (*) in the biblical text, look for a footnote about that text.

The second set of notes is a little more confusing at first because there are no sentences or even words. Instead you see abbreviated titles to various books of the Bible followed by chapter and verse numbers. These are cross-references. The editors of your Bible have identified for you other passages from the Bible that connect in some way with the passage you are currently reading.

Let's look at the first cross-reference. It reads this way: "a Gn 2,1.4: Pss 8,4; 38–39; 90,2; Wis 11,17…" and so on. The little *a* at the beginning matches a little *a* in the text you are reading. See it floating above the line after "the heavens and the earth" in the first verse of Genesis 1? If you take the time to look up all the passages listed in this note, you will discover many more references to the creation of heaven and earth in the Bible. And you will have so much more material to feed your meditation and prayer on this first verse of the Bible.

At this point you may be wondering how I know such wonderful mysteries. No magic really. I found an explanation of all this in the introductory material. Just look at the page bearing the roman numeral xii.

THE JERUSALEM BIBLE

The Jerusalem Bible also has two sets of notes, but the editors have arranged them differently. At the bottom of the right-page of biblical text are notes explaining something about the text you are reading. For example, on the first page of Genesis you will see this at the bottom: "1 a. This narrative….." The number 1 refers, of course, to the first chapter of Genesis. The letter *a* matches the little *a* at the end of the subheading in the text. All this means that this first footnote tells you something about the portion of Genesis with the subheading "The first account of the creation."

Where are the cross-references in the Jerusalem Bible? They are in the margins on the right and the left edges of the book as it lies open in front of you. Personally I find this arrangement a little more accessible since the relevant passages are easy to see.

REVISED STANDARD VERSION: CATHOLIC EDITION

If you turn to the first chapter of Genesis, you will find two sets of notes. They are sitting there below the right-hand column of most pages. The first set of notes is introduced by a small letter corresponding to a small letter in the text of the Bible on the page. The first note reads: "a Or: When God began to create". This note presents you with an alternative translation of the first line of the Bible. If we translate the line according to this alternative reading, the first thing God does is speak the words, "Let there be light." And that offers a fascinating parallel with the first line of John's Gospel, "In the beginning was the word." This, of course, is the point of the second set of notes introduced by the citation: 1.1 and then referring you to John 1:1.

Such notes have great value for leading you to new and deeper insights about the text of the Bible you happen to be reading at the time. I can only encourage you to get into the habit of taking full advantage of the notes in your Bible. It will definitely add a richer dimension to your reading.

Now you are equipped to go out and shop for a Bible that is just right for you. The important thing is that you find at least one translation of the Bible that you find appealing. And just remember that the same translation of the Bible may appear in many different editions, each one offering a little something different to help you get the most out of your reading.

Here is a handy summary of things to keep in mind when you look for a Bible:

+ Keep reading until you find a translation with which you are comfortable.
+ Make certain it offers all the books of the Bible, including additions to Esther and Daniel.
+ Look for an edition of your translation that best serves your interests. You may want a simple edition or you may want one with a lot of extras.

And here is a handy summary of things to help you get more out of reading your Bible:

+ Get into the habit of scanning each page of your Bible for markers alerting you to the fine print on the page.
+ Read those footnotes.
+ Take the time to look up at least some of the other Bible passages listed in the cross-references.

PRAYING WITH THE BIBLE

If you read Revelation 10:8–11, you will discover a fascinating scene. John is directed by a voice from heaven to eat a scroll handed to him by angel. He does so, finding it sweet in his mouth but bitter in his stomach. The message seems to be that receiving the word of God is a pleasant thing but putting it into practice can be a challenge. Have you found this true for you? Think about the "sweet" passages of the Bible you have discovered over the years. Now think about the challenges each one presents for you. Offer a prayer to God asking for the strength to truly live out the word of God in your life. You might even find it helpful to make bookmarks for your favorite passages. Write on each one what you found sweet about it and what you found bitter.

FOR REFLECTION

Invite members of the Bible study group to tell the story about how they got their Bibles. Ask them to "sell" their Bibles to the rest of the group. What are the most attractive features? What are their favorite passages to read. Make it a real show-and-tell experience.

Choose a passage from the Bible. If you have trouble deciding where to start, try "The Wedding at Cana" in 2:1–11 of John's Gospel.

Invite the members of the group to read the notes their editions include on this passage. How do they help them understand the passage? How do they help make the passage more vivid?

Divide among the group the cross-references on this passage. Ask each member to look up his or her reference and read it aloud to the rest. Talk about the insights each reference contributes to the reading. How does each reference help them appreciate the passage on a deeper level?

CHAPTER TWO: THE TREE OF LIFE

Years ago the title page of a book would feature a sketch of a gateway, suggesting that beyond the title page the reader entered a new place created by the author of the book. The title page of your Bible surely qualifies as a gateway to a new place. But this entrance leads to a very special place because God is the author. If you let this idea sink in for a moment, it becomes almost impossible to resist turning that title page to see what lies beyond it.

This chapter will give you an overview of what lies beyond the title page of your Bible. My hope is to give you a sense of the way the Bible progresses from start to finish. Having this overview will make it easier for you to look at the various chapters that make up the Bible because you will have a sense of where each part of the Bible fits within the whole.

THE BEGINNING AND THE END

Perhaps you have never thought about it but the Bible begins and ends with the same image, the image of a tree. Of course, the tree of the knowledge of good and evil gets all the attention in the Adam and Eve account. We all know about the way the serpent tricked the two of them into eating from the tree. And we all know the consequences of eating from that knowledge tree. But what about that other tree in the Garden of Eden: the tree of life?

It's difficult to determine if Adam and Eve ate from this tree before the Fall, but they certainly wanted to eat from it after the Fall. Why? Because they were now destined for the grave and this tree offered them everlasting life. But I often think how kind God was not to allow them to eat from the tree of life so soon after they ate from that knowledge tree. If they had done so, they might have been subject to suffering and the anticipation of death forever.

God graciously spared them such a fate by keeping them away from the tree of life. But interestingly enough God does not get rid of the tree (a possible option, you must admit). Instead, God puts a guard along the way that leads to the tree of life. This suggests to me that God was already planning to provide a way to get back to that tree. And of course, that is exactly why Jesus Christ came into the world. Jesus is the one who leads the way back to the tree of life with sure steps. You have probably seen artistic representations of the cross of Jesus beautifully expressing this truth. The cross is transformed into the tree of life.

†

Saint Jerome was not the first to translate the Bible into Latin. Latin translations of the Greek New Testament were circulating in southern France and northern Africa, old provinces of the Roman Empire, almost two centuries before Jerome began his work.

The final book of the Bible picks up this same theme. In the final chapter of Revelation the tree of life is featured once again "with its twelve kinds of fruit, producing its fruit each month" (Revelation 22:2 in the New Revised Standard Version). Who could resist such a variety of fruit? And it produces such wonderful flavors all year long! But can anyone get beyond that swirling sword of fire guarding the way to the tree of life? The answer is yes. Look at verse 14 of that final chapter. It says that the blessed who wash their robes have access to the tree. In other words, all the people who believe in Jesus have access to the tree. Jesus certainly has access to it, and anyone who follows him does, too.

This image of the tree of life serves as a wonderful reminder of the Bible's main theme: there is life in listening to God. If Adam and Eve had listened to God in the first place, they would have been spared a lot of pain and suffering. But instead they chose to ignore God's word. And ignoring the word of God is the prelude to trouble. But fortunately for us the Word entered our world to lead us to eternal life. John's Gospel expresses it so beautifully:

> For God so loved the world that he gave his only Son,
> so that everyone who believes in him may not perish
> but may have eternal life. (John 3:16, NRSV)

With this understanding of the beginning and the end of the Bible, we can think of everything in the middle as contributing in some way to our learning about how to get back to the tree of life. Interestingly enough, as if to remind us about the tree of life, there are references to fruit trees throughout the rest of the Bible. Think of the tree planted by streams of water and producing fruit in season (Psalm 1) or the tree our Lord speaks of that is known by its good fruit (Matthew 7:17).

†

The tradition of breaking up the Bible into numbered chapters probably started in the lecture halls of the great universities that sprang up in Europe during the thirteenth century.

Whenever I read the creation account of Genesis 1–3, I am struck by the fact that our gracious God put fruit trees in this world. This goes for fig trees, too, in spite of the fact that Adam and Eve turned to a fig tree to make their famous leafy coverings. I wonder if God intended fruit trees to serve as a reminder in this world of the Garden of Eden.

THE MIDDLE

Let's look at the books that stand between the beginning and the end of the Bible. If you are reading from a Roman Catholic Bible, there are another forty-five books in the Old Testament and another twenty-six in the New Testament. That is a lot of material to consider. But fortunately our printed Bibles provide us with a table of contents to help us make our way through all these books.

THE OLD TESTAMENT

A standard way to organize the books of the Old Testament is by dividing it into the Pentateuch, historical books, wisdom books and prophetic books. Let's take a look at each of these four main groups. This is going to be a simplified overview. But the point is to give you a feel for the way the Bible develops the theme of how important it is to listen to God.

THE PENTATEUCH

This is admittedly a pretty strange sounding word. The reason it sounds foreign to our ears is because it is a Greek word meaning "five scrolls," specifically the five scrolls (in book form today) that stand at the beginning of the Bible. Taken together these five books serve as the foundation for all the books that follow. Others include these five books under the title Torah, a Hebrew word meaning "law" or "instruction." It serves well as a title for these books since their most prominent feature is the great narrative about Moses giving the people the Law of God on Mount Sinai.

The basic theme of the Pentateuch is that people ought to be listening to God. But people usually end up listening to something else and that gets them into trouble. How much trouble? Think of the flood in the time of Noah. Think of the years the people spent in bondage in Egypt. But God never stops connecting with people. Finally the people listen to God's servant Moses who leads them out of Egypt (*Exodus* means "the road out") to the mountain of God. At Mt. Sinai the people make a solemn promise to remain loyal to God and then begin their journey back to the Promised Land, the land of their fathers, Abraham, Isaac and Jacob.

THE HISTORICAL BOOKS

After the Pentateuch (or Torah) come the books that record how things worked out in history between God and Israel. Basically it is pretty much the story of the people's failure to listen to God. But God keeps trying, even giving them special leaders to steer them in the right direction. The leaders' names make up the titles of many of the books in this section of the Bible: Joshua, Judges, Samuel, Kings, Ezra, Nehemiah and members of the Maccabee family. There are also some books in this section that feature people who actually did listen to God: Ruth, Judith, Esther, Tobit. Finally Chronicles 1 and 2 give a kind of idealized picture of the whole history.

THE WISDOM BOOKS

At this point in our overview of the Bible, we are familiar with the basic outline of Israel's relationship with God. The Wisdom Books come next. They can be understood as applying the lesson of the previous books to our daily lives. Some of the books in this section are basically collections of guidelines for everyday life as God's people. In this group we can include Proverbs, Ecclesiastes, Sirach and, of course, the Book of Wisdom. A special book in this section is the book of Job, which follows one man's inner journey toward a deeper relationship with God. Everyone is familiar with at least a few of the Psalms. This beautiful poetry captures nearly every emotion touching the lives of people in their relationship with God. The Song of Songs captures the love between God and people in the lyrics of beautiful love poetry.

THE PROPHETS

The Old Testament in Christian Bibles concludes with the oracles of the prophets because they point the way to the fulfillment of God's plan in Jesus Christ. In this section there are three major prophets (Isaiah, Jeremiah and Ezekiel) and twelve minor prophets. If you seek a helpful image for a prophet, consider the one offered in Amos 7:1–10 where the prophet seems to be compared to a plumb line set in the midst of the people of Israel. Just as a plumb line reveals whether or not a wall meets the standards of the architect, so the message of Amos reveals whether or not the people meet the standards of God. The prophets challenged the people to remain faithful to God. But because the people failed to listen, the prophets looked to the future when God would send someone who would at last lead the people in the right direction. For Christians, of course, that someone is Jesus Christ.

THE NEW TESTAMENT

The New Testament carries forward the message of salvation initiated in the Old Testament. Its main theme is that Jesus Christ is the Son of God and the one who fulfilled the work of salvation begun by his Father. We can view the books in this part of the Bible in much the same way we viewed the books of the Old Testament.

THE FOUR GOSPELS

The four Gospels do for the New Testament what the Pentateuch does for the Old Testament: they establish its foundation. The Gospels proclaim the truth of Jesus Christ who fulfilled the plan of salvation already set in motion from the beginning of time. Each of the four evangelists proclaims the gospel, but each one does so in a way that is unique. You are probably most familiar with this part of the Bible.

ACTS OF THE APOSTLES

To carry on our comparison with the Old Testament, Acts records how things worked out in history just as the Historical Books do in the Old Testament. In Acts we witness the work of Jesus Christ continued by his apostles, now empowered by the gift of the Holy Spirit. Where the people of Israel often failed, the apostles were successful. They were faithful to the commission Jesus gave them before he ascended into heaven. By the end of Acts, the gospel is being proclaimed in Rome, the political center of the Mediterranean world at that time.

THE LETTERS

These letters of the New Testament can be applied to our daily lives in much the same way we can apply the Wisdom and Prophetic Books of the Old Testament. They inform us about the efforts of Paul and others to steer the Christian community toward the truth of Jesus Christ. This was not an easy task since the early communities were confronted with a world that was, if not downright hostile, at least at odds with the ideals embraced by those who were baptized in the Lord. And of course, in many respects their struggles are the struggles of Christians in any age.

I think organizing the Bible around the theme of the tree of life can be very helpful. From the moment Adam and Eve left the garden, God was working to guide them back. When someone asked the rabbis what God was doing since creation, they said God was busy making ladders between earth and heaven. The rabbis had it right. From the point of view of the biblical authors there is no question that God is invested in our spiritual well-being. The real question is whether people are equally invested in responding to God. The books in the center of the Bible develop this theme from many different angles.

This quick walking tour of the Bible can by no means do justice to the rich message of the biblical books. But it does at least provide you with one way of viewing the many books of the Bible as an integral whole. The main point I wish to make here is that the Bible has been given to us by God for our spiritual benefit. Through its powerful message, God seeks to give us every advantage in our spiritual journey. By reading about the failures and successes of those who walked the journey before us, we gain some advantage for our own journey. And, of course, to that end the Christian Bible places all the focus on Jesus Christ who is the way, the truth and the life.

†

One of the most spectacular finds at the caves of Qumran near the Dead Sea was a complete scroll of the Book of Isaiah on prepared animal skin called parchment. It measures 10½ inches from top to bottom. Unrolled, it is almost 25 feet in length. The entire text of Isaiah appears in 54 columns with an average of 30 lines apiece. It dates from the early first century before the birth of Jesus.

Some helpful suggestions for getting started as a Bible reader:

- † Begin with passages of the Bible that are familiar to you.
- † Start with brief segments first, then move on to larger ones.
- † Take notes, writing down insights and observations as you go along.
- † Try to keep the general outline of the Bible in mind as you read.
- † Take a moment to mentally picture where the book you are reading from fits into the big picture.

PRAYING WITH THE BIBLE

If you read Luke 4:16–20, you will discover how familiar Jesus was with the prophecies of Isaiah. Jesus returned to his hometown and was given the honor of reading the Scripture passage for the service. They handed him a scroll. If this scroll was anything like the scroll of Isaiah found in cave four of Qumran, it would have been about twenty inches high and thirty feet long. This means Jesus had to unroll the scroll almost to the end to find the passage he read from chapter 61. Imagine being that familiar with a biblical book. He must have prayed with that passage many times.

Choose a passage from your favorite biblical book. Read it slowly. After you read, stop and reflect about it. Write down your ideas and insights. Then try to compose a prayer based on your ideas and insights. You will be surprised how many of your own personal prayers you can accumulate this way in just a short time.

FOR REFLECTION

Many computer programs today offer a "favorites" label on the menu line. This provides users with a convenient way to access quickly the websites they like the most. What Bible passages would members of the group include among their favorites? Invite them to read from their favorites and explain why they like them so much. See if you can identify favorites from each of the main sections of the Bible outlined in this chapter.

Very popular items around the time of Saint Francis were Bibles presenting a scene from the Bible and then pairing it with a scene from everyday life. The reader learned a valuable lesson by applying the lesson of the Bible scene with the scene from life. Ask members of the group to make connections between their favorite passages and something from their own experience or current events. What insights does this activity lead to for them?

Ask members of the group to choose a favorite psalm or section from the Book of Proverbs for the next meeting. Ask them to set aside a certain amount of time each day to read and pray over the same passage. Then ask them to write down what insights they gained each day. The next time the group meets, invite the members to talk about their experience and their insights with the rest of the group.

CHAPTER THREE: FOCUS ON THE PEOPLE

Now that you have a Bible or two and have a feeling for the way it is organized, you are ready to open its pages and begin reading. But how does a person begin reading the Bible? Where to start? At the beginning? At the end? Somewhere in between? My own feeling is that people can start anywhere they like because the biblical work is such that no matter what portion of the book you read there are spiritual lessons to be learned.

By God's grace, the books of the Bible were written by a variety of people from many different backgrounds and periods of time. We know who many of them were. There was Moses from the period of the Exodus, David from the earliest days of the kings, and prophets like Isaiah from the eighth century before the time of Jesus. The New Testament authors may be better known to us: the four evangelists, Paul, Peter and John.

But all these authors, whether in the Old Testament or the New, have something in common. They all put the greatest value on a right relationship with God. And that, I believe, is the key to why they wrote what they did. They wanted to help us get close to God, too. And so, when reading the Bible, I think the most fruitful question to ask is, What am I learning about my relationship with God? And one of the best ways to find out is by paying attention to the people in the book.

Biblical narrative does not devote a lot of lines to setting the stage or describing the scenes. In this respect the literature of the Bible is quite different from the literature we find on the best-seller shelves today. What the biblical authors do concentrate on are people. Choose any page from the Bible and you will find yourself reading about somebody: a man, a woman, a prophet, a king, a disciple and count-less others.

So, as you read from the Bible, ask yourself, What is the author telling me about the people in this biblical account? Are they listen-ing to God, or not? Do they value what God values, or not? What are the reasons they do what they do? Are they interested in personal advantage? Are they interested in serving God?

†

The early Christians appear to have been the first group in antiquity to make extensive use of the book format. We know this from copies of the Bible dating back to the second and third centuries of our era. Almost everyone else was still using scrolls at that time.

There are characters in the Bible who clearly serve as models of faith. Mary the mother of our Lord is an obvious choice. Her words, "Let it be done to me according to your word" challenge all of us to strive much harder in our own responses.

Other characters represent the opposite side of the spectrum. Think of Judas, who could not tear himself away from the lure of money, even going so far as to betray the Lord for a handful of silver coins.

Let's take a close look at some further examples:

A MAN AND A TREE

In the previous chapter we talked about the tree of life, so why not begin our focus on biblical characters with an account that involves a tree? In this case the featured tree is a kind of fig tree called a sycamore. And the character is, as you may have already guessed, Zacchaeus. You will find the account of his conversion in Luke 19:1–10. We will be reading his story from the NRSV.

At the start, Zacchaeus seems an unlikely candidate for a list of famous believers in the New Testament. We learn, first of all, that he was a tax collector. So he was more than likely in the employ of Rome, gathering revenue for the empire from his fellow citizens. It seems that his interest would be entirely in material things.

Furthermore, Zacchaeus seems to admit to a habit of cheating his customers. When he comes down from the tree, he announces to Jesus "... if I have defrauded anyone of anything, I will pay back four times as much."

A third strike against Zacchaeus is the fact he is rich. Readers of Luke have already met the infamous Dives, the name tradition has given to the "rich man" in the story of poor Lazarus (Luke 16:19–31). Things turned out very badly for Dives who could never be bothered to reach beyond his table full of food to offer even a crumb to the poor man at his gate. So when we discover that Zacchaeus is also rich we might expect to hear still another story about someone blinded by the material things in life.

A fascinating detail in the account about Zacchaeus is his small stature. Here we get one of those rare glimpses of the physical appearance of someone in the Bible. Now we know why he had to climb a tree in order to get a look at Jesus! But at the same time we discover something in this little tax collector that makes him a lot bigger than so many other characters in the Gospels: he wants to see Jesus.

†
Study Bibles are nothing new. The original Douay-Rheims Bible (1582–1610) had so many notes and extra material that it took up three volumes!

Luke does not explore the inner thoughts of Zacchaeus. But doesn't it seem possible there was already a yearning inside of him for something more? Imagine his face when Jesus looks up at him and calls his name!

This passage that seemed predictably bleak at the start takes a sudden turn for the better. So much so that Jesus can joyfully announce, "Today salvation has come to this house, because he too is a son of Abraham. For the Son of Man came to seek out and to save the lost."

For Zacchaeus that sycamore tree served as a kind of tree of life. He climbed up that tree as a cheating tax collector and he came down from that tree a model of faith for us. Zacchaeus also teaches us something about real values. He exchanged his attachment to material things for an attachment to the things of heaven.

THE RICH MAN

Now let's consider a passage about another rich man. You can find the story in Mark 10:17–22. But unlike Zacchaeus, this man finds attachment to the things of this world an almost insurmountable barrier to faith.

His story begins with so much promise, quite unlike the story of Zacchaeus. Mark tells us the man "ran up" to Jesus. We can almost see the excitement in his eyes, perhaps even anticipating that Jesus will congratulate him for his devotion to the commandments.

But Jesus challenges him to make one more step along the road to perfection. He tells him "go, sell what you own, and give the money to the poor, and you will have treasure in heaven; then come, follow me." Now there is a change in the man. His enthusiasm is replaced with shock and then grief. All he can do now is slowly walk away.

Why does he find it so difficult to accept what Jesus offers him? Why does he walk away sad? Is he struggling with the idea of putting his possessions aside to embrace the kingdom of heaven? Did he ever return to Jesus, ready to put all aside to follow him? Part of me wants to believe he did.

As we read this account we cannot escape wondering about our own relationship with God. Is there some attachment to the things of earth that keeps us from getting closer to God? Such questions may help us in our own journey of faith.

JOB

Job's patience is the stuff of legend. He remains loyal to God in spite of everything that happens to him. And everyone would agree, an awful lot happened to him. But I'm not going to concentrate on Job's patience because I think Job's patient endurance of his suffering is only part of the story. What I find really impressive about him is the change we see in him in the final chapter of the book.

In the final scene, God restores Job's family. He has seven sons and three daughters just as he did at the beginning. But there is a difference. In fact, it turns out to be a very big difference.

In the first chapter of Job we never see Job with his daughters. But in the final chapter Job gives his daughters a great deal of attention. In fact, we discover that Job is the one who names each one. See if you can find that in any other book of the Bible!

It seems the name he gives each one reflects her special kind of beauty. Since the eldest daughter apparently had soft skin or perhaps because of the soft sounds she made, Job named her Jemimah, meaning "dove." Job named the middle daughter Keziah, denoting a precious perfume. Did he find her so sweet? The youngest daughter may have had beautiful eyes because Job named her Keren-happuch, denoting a kind of eye shadow or mascara. Whatever the reason for the names Job gave his daughters, there is absolutely no doubt that Job noticed them. In their father's eyes they were the most beautiful girls in the world.

And more than that, Job gave each one an inheritance that matched whatever each of his sons received. Any commentary will tell you this was way beyond the norm in those days. It says a lot about the way Job looked at his world. Clearly he saw everything as a gift from God.

None of us may suffer the way Job did. But all of us can decide right now to look at this world the way he did.

FIVE COURAGEOUS SISTERS

In the days of Moses a certain Israelite had five daughters—Mahlah, Noah, Hoglah, Milcah and Tirzah. It is not likely you ever heard of them before. But their story is worth reading. You will find it in Numbers 27. We will use the NRSV.

When the time came to divide up the Promised Land among the tribes of Israel, these five sisters came forward. Their father had no sons, and so it looked like there would be no inheritance for his family. But these steadfast sisters had a special request.

> Why should the name of our father be taken away from his clan because he had no son? Give to us a possession among our father's brothers ...

There it was. They were asking Moses to break with tradition and allow daughters to inherit land. But there was more here than a plea for inheritance. These five women, unlike the entire first generation to leave Egypt, were confident that they would be entering the Promised Land. They had faith. In fact, their faith was greater than the faith of half of their own tribe of Manasseh who were satisfied to settle in land east of the Jordan River rather than wait for an inheritance in the Promised Land.

So unique was their request that Moses had to take their case to God. And God's answer?

> And the Lord spoke to Moses, saying: The daughters of
> Zelophehad are right in what they are saying; you shall
> indeed let them possess an inheritance among their
> father's brothers and pass the inheritance of their father
> on to them.

Of course, these five sisters play only a minor role in the great story of Israel's journey to the Promised Land. But from them we learn a great deal about the true significance of the Promised Land. They understood that it was a gift from God to those who believed, whether male or female.

PETER THE APOSTLE

Some characters in the Bible are quite complex. Consider the apostle Peter, especially as his story is told in the Gospel of John. Peter is silent at first, not saying a word even as he hears Jesus announce to him that his name will be changed from Simon to Peter.

When we do hear his first words in John's Gospel, Peter asks, "Lord, to whom can we go? You have the words of eternal life." (John 6:68, NRSV). This seems to reveal a deep spiritual yearning in Peter's heart.

But then comes that threefold denial of any association with Jesus. After this scene the fourth evangelist is silent once again about the inner thoughts of this apostle. John does not even tell us, as the other Gospels do, that Peter went away and wept when he heard the cock crow.

But in the final chapter of John's Gospel, Peter replaces his denials with three assertions of deep love for the Lord. We are even told that Peter will give glory to God by dying for his Lord. Little wonder that in the Acts of the Apostles we see Peter preaching boldly the gospel of Jesus without a trace of the doubt that once cast shadows on his journey of faith.

Complex people like Peter appear quite frequently in the Bible. Consider, for example, the story of Abraham and Sarah struggling to believe that God's promise of a son really will be fulfilled. Or the story of David as he struggles to remain faithful to the ideals of kingship in Israel. If we apply these accounts to our own lives, we will probably discover that such complex people are very much like ourselves as we struggle to believe in God and to remain loyal to the ideals of our faith.

I encourage people to make a list of favorite characters from the Bible. Here is my own list. I have them in order of appearance. Read their stories and see what you think. Then you may want to work up a list of your own.

NOAH	Genesis 5:29—9:29	He walked with God.
SHIPHRAH AND PUAH	Exodus 1:15–21	They listened to God rather than Pharaoh.
CALEB	Numbers 13—14	He believed in God's word.
MAHLAH AND SISTERS	Numbers 27	They trusted in God's promise.
DEBORAH	Judges 4	She spoke the word of God.
HANNAH	1 Samuel 1–2	She prayed for the gift of life.
ABIGAIL	1 Samuel 25	She called David to faith in God.
URIAH	2 Samuel 11	He was a faithful servant of God.
OBADIAH	1 Kings 18	He risked his life for God's prophets.
THE SHUNAMMITE	2 Kings 4	She valued God over all else.
THE HEBREW GIRL	2 Kings 5	She taught others about God.
RUTH	Book of Ruth	She was loyal to God's people.
ESTHER	Book of Esther	She saved her people.
JUDITH	Book of Judith	She saved her people.
THE CANAANITE	Matthew 15:21–28	Jesus spoke of her great faith.
MARY OF BETHANY	John 12:1–8	She anointed Jesus.
MARY MAGDALENE	John 20	She announced the Lord's resurrection.
DORCAS	Acts 9:36–39	She was full of good works.

Some helpful hints:
† Focus on the people in each biblical account.
† Look for clues about a person's spiritual character.
† Does this person bring God into his or her life?
† Is this person inclined to think of this world as a gift from God?
† Are the things of this world an obstacle for this person's spiritual life?

PRAYING WITH THE BIBLE

Jesus ben Sirach includes in his book a wonderful review of the famous people of the Bible. You will find the beginning of it in Sirach 44. The review concludes with Sirach 49. What this seasoned teacher intended to do with this cast of biblical characters is to hold them up as models of wisdom. Each of them walked the journey of faith, though some met with greater success on that journey than others. One way you might use this list as a resource for prayer is by choosing one figure and reading what Sirach has to say about him. Then imagine what Sirach might say about you if you were inserted into this portion of his book. How would you compare to the biblical figure? How would you be different?

You may be wondering, What about the famous women of the Bible? Sirach did not include any in his list because he was focused on "our fathers" (Sirach 44:1). But not to worry. If you look at the larger story of many of these famous men, you will find famous women along side them. Think of Sarah with Abraham, Rebecca with Isaac, Hannah with Samuel, or Abigail with David. Another way to balance this prayer is to look at the final chapter of the Book of Proverbs. It offers a wonderful description of the perfect spouse who is a blessing to all she meets. She may even represent Wisdom. As you read about her, put yourself into the chapter. How would it read if this were a description of you and your relationship with God? What blessings do you bring into the lives of those you meet?

FOR REFLECTION

Choose a scene from the Bible, maybe one of the scenes we looked at in this chapter. Ask the group to imagine they are in charge of casting for a production of the scene. Who would they choose to play the different characters? They can choose from people in the film industry or from their own circle of friends. The process should generate an interesting discussion because it will reveal the different ways people "see" the biblical characters.

CHAPTER FOUR: FIRST IMPRESSIONS

We worry about doing something for the first time. Almost everyone can remember the first day of school. There were so many unknowns. So many new things to learn about. Even the simplest tasks were major projects because we had to face them for the first time.

Meeting people for the first time can make us especially uneasy. Will we like them? Will they like us? What will they think about the way we look, the way we talk, the things we wear? Eventually, of course, things have a way of working themselves out. As we get to know people better, we become more comfortable with them. And later on it is fascinating to compare what we know of them with the impression they made on us at the first meeting.

We can do the same sort of thing with the people we meet in the Bible. We can ask ourselves what kind of impression they make on us the first time we read about them in the Bible. Do we like them? Do we feel close to them? What do we find impressive about them? Do they give us valuable lessons about our faith journey? Or do they seem the sort of people that would lead us away from God rather than closer?

I find it helpful to pay attention to whether my first impressions about a character change or remain the same as I read more and more about them. I ask myself why my thinking about them changed or remained the same. I find that it can lead to some deeper insights about the faith journey. And it certainly helps me get even more out of reading the Bible.

Let's consider a few examples:

PAUL

Paul is an obvious choice to practice this approach for the first time, because we are all so familiar with his story. Our first impression of the apostle Paul (when he was still known as Saul) is a negative one. After all, the first time we meet him he is busy persecuting the church. As he confesses in his letter to the Galatians, he actually tried to destroy the church because he was so zealous for the tradition of his ancestors (Galatians 1:13–14).

†

Johannes Gutenberg's printed Bible of 1455 was a real innovation. But Gutenberg was also a traditionalist. His printed Bible imitated the hand-copied Bibles of the day—two columns to each page. Many printed Bibles today preserve this tradition.

But this first impression is soon replaced by feelings of admiration and respect for Paul as we read about his conversion, his preaching of the gospel and the hardships he endured for the faith. The faith journey of this apostle to the Gentiles actually becomes a source of inspiration, challenging us to think about what conversion we need to make in our own lives so that we can serve the Lord more faithfully.

KING SAUL

King Saul of Israel is another good subject for this sort of approach to reading the Bible. His first impression is definitely a positive one. He is chosen by God and anointed by the prophet Samuel. He is an able leader, defending his people against the Philistine army. But slowly we begin to realize that this able leader has no appreciation for the spiritual dimension of his kingship. He is more impressed with popular approval than with the anointing given him by a prophet of God. We never see him at prayer. He finds more security in the proximity of a spear than in a relationship with God.

A good sampling of Saul's true character can be found in the famous battle scene between David and Goliath (1 Samuel 17). David announces that with God's help he can defeat Goliath. But Saul insists on David wearing the standard battle gear of the day: a bronze helmet, a coat of armor and a heavy sword. It is amusing to think of young David struggling to move around under the weight of all that armor. But such physical resources for protection mean far more to Saul than any appeal to the God of Israel. Even David's victory over Goliath with a single stone does not move Saul to greater faith in God.

And so our favorable impression of Saul at first meeting gradually fades as we see him fail over and over again to trust in the God who called him to kingship.

REBEKAH

Some characters are a little more challenging, because different or even opposite motives can be ascribed to the things they do. Rebekah is one of the most intriguing characters in the Book of Genesis. We first meet her in Genesis 24 where she is literally the answer to a prayer. Abraham sent his most trusted servant back to his home country to find a wife for his son Isaac. When the servant arrives at his destination, he begins praying to the God of Abraham asking for assistance in his mission. His prayer is not even finished when Rebekah appears on the scene.

†

If you are looking for saintly advice on reading the Old Testament, Saint Jerome recommended the Psalms as a good place to start, followed by Proverbs because of its sound advice for everyday living.

So we could think of Rebekah as the answer to a prayer, making our first impression of her definitely a positive one. But does she remain an ideal character? Difficulties arise in the famous scene from Genesis 27 where Rebekah dresses up Jacob to feel and smell like his brother Esau so that Isaac will give Jacob his blessing.

If Rebekah is motivated solely by favoritism, her character has taken a definite turn for the worse. She is deceiving her poor blind husband in order to give her favorite son Jacob an advantage over his older brother Esau who should rightfully be the one to receive the blessing.

But I have always wondered if Rebekah's motivations were higher. After all, she has overheard Isaac speak about his wanting to bless Esau before he dies. But she was told by God before the twins were born that the older son should be the servant of the younger son. Could she be thinking, "Do I want Isaac to die never recognizing that Jacob is the one who is heir in the eyes of God?"

We might even regard Isaac's blindness as a gift from God so that he will learn to see by an inner light rather than the light of the sun. If this is so, then we could understand Rebekah as actually helping her husband see more clearly on a spiritual level.

She resorts to deception only because she is desperate, believing time is running out since she overheard Isaac speak about his imminent death. If this is Rebekah's motive, then her good character remains secure.

Either interpretation is possible, though admittedly the first one is the more common one. But in any case, there is a spiritual lesson to be learned whether Rebekah's motives are pure or questionable. Either Rebekah is someone we can admire for her devotion to her husband's spiritual welfare, or Rebekah is a negative model, showing how personal agendas can get in the way of our spiritual progress. Whatever lesson we draw from her story, Rebekah teaches us and gives us valuable insights into our own relationship with God.

NICODEMUS

If you look up this character in a Bible dictionary, you are likely to be told that little is known about him. While it is true his story is not a major one in the Gospel of John, we do know enough about him to put his name on the list of biblical characters who can help us on our faith journey.

At first Nicodemus came to learn from Jesus at night. John does not give us an explicit reason for this man's interest in avoiding the light. But we cannot be too far off the mark if we attribute his night visits to caution. After all, he was a notable authority on the law and would therefore not have been too anxious to have his night classes a matter of public knowledge. At least not at the start.

But on the day Jesus dies on the cross, Nicodemus comes forward into the light of day. He and Joseph of Arimathea—another secret disciple of Jesus—take the body of Jesus and prepare it for burial. Nicodemus brings with him costly ointments for the ritual, and they place Jesus' body in a new tomb. Do they simply want to honor in a special way the body of someone they respected? Or are they thinking this dignified burial was the only proper way to anticipate that Jesus would rise from the dead as he had promised?

Whatever Nicodemus is thinking when we last see him in John's Gospel, his journey from the darkness of night to the light of day gives us encouragement in our own journeys. Just like Nicodemus, we should make some measurable progress in our devotion to the Lord.

The examples above should help you get started doing this sort of reflection on Scripture on your own. I think you will find it as rewarding as I do. Just remember, this is not a test. You need not worry about whether your feelings about a character match what others think. What does matter is whether your reflection on a biblical figure helps you understand you own relationship with God a little better.

If you are looking for a place to start, why not begin with the genealogy in Luke or Matthew? Pick out a few names, read their stories and learn from their successes, or maybe even their struggles.

Some helpful hints:

   † Make a note, at least a mental one, about your impressions of a biblical character the first time you read about him or her in the Bible.
   † See if your first impression changes at all as you discover more about this character.
   † Look for the faith lesson in this character. Does it offer you something you can apply to your own spiritual journey?
   † You do not need to find the first time a character *actually* appears in the Bible to apply this technique effectively. What matters is where *you* first meet the character.

PRAYING WITH THE BIBLE

Psalm 139 begins with these beautiful lines:

> O LORD, you have searched me and known me.
> You know when I sit down and when I rise up;
>   you discern my thoughts from far away. (NRSV)

As the psalmist recognizes, we are entirely transparent to God. That might make us uneasy, unless of course, we try to live our lives as servants of God. And if we do, then we never have to worry about what kind of first impression we make on others.

Read Psalm 139 slowly and reflectively. Let its message sink into your heart. Do you see anything within your heart you would like to change, something others cannot see but God does see? Pray that God will help you make that change.

FOR REFLECTION

Read aloud the description of King Saul in 1 Samuel 9:1–2. If this were all the group had to go on, what would be their impression of Saul? Ask them to think about how his story might have turned out based on what they think of him in this reading alone. What are similar stories from their own experiences?

Read the passage from Job 2:11–13 about the three friends who come to visit with Job. As the group listens, ask them to try to picture each friend. What might the three friends have been feeling as they sat with Job for seven days? Ask the group to think about the friends they would choose to have with them in times of trouble.

From the Bible the rabbis identified twenty-three remarkable women in Israel and eight remarkable women from the nations. Here are their two lists. Some of the women may not be familiar to you so I have noted where you can find their stories in the Bible.

Twenty-three remarkable women in Israel:
† Sarah
† Rebekah
† Rachel
† Leah
† Jochebed (Exodus 6:20)
† Miriam
† Deborah
† the wife of Manoah (Judges 13)
† Hannah (1 Samuel 1—2)
† Abigail (1 Samuel 25)
† the woman of Tekoa (2 Samuel 14)
† the widow helped by Elijah (1 Kings 17)
† the Shunammite woman (2 Kings 4:8–37)
† Huldah (2 Kings 22:14–20)
† Naomi (Ruth)
† Jehosheba (2 Kings 11:2)

† the woman helped by Elisha (2 Kings 4:1–7)
† Esther
† the five daughters of Zelophehad (Numbers 27:1–11)

Eight remarkable women from the nations who are mentioned in the Bible:

† Hagar (Genesis 16)
† Asenath (Genesis 41:50–52)
† Zipporah (Exodus 2:21–22)
† Shiphrah (Exodus 1:15–21)
† Puah (Exodus 1:15–21)
† Rahab (Joshua 2)
† Jael (Judges 4:17–22)
† Ruth

What reasons do you think the rabbis would have offered to include each woman in the list? Do you agree with their choices? Are there any others you would add to the list?

CHAPTER FIVE: LISTENING CAREFULLY

Have you ever noticed that we almost never get a description of someone in the Bible? I mean what he or she actually looked like: the color of her eyes, or the shape of his nose. Since we cannot see the faces of the people in the Bible we have to pay special attention to what they say. That will give us some idea about who they are. And fortunately for us people in the Bible do a lot of talking. In fact, the greater part of any biblical book is the spoken word.

Of course, we hear a lot of words every day—on the radio, on the television, on the phone, at work, in the office, in school and at home. But we also screen out a lot of what we hear. How could anyone process the countless number of words we take in each day? But when it comes to the Bible we will miss out on a lot if we screen out what people say. Think of their words as a kind of special lens that allows us to see the inner person that remains invisible on the surface.

Let's consider some examples that will illustrate what I mean.

EVE

We have just one line from Eve after she and Adam leave the Garden of Eden. It is what she says when she names her first son. She says, in the English of the New Revised Standard Version, "I have produced a man with the help of the LORD" (Genesis 4:1). The footnotes will clue you in on the detail that the Hebrew word translated "produced" sounds a lot like the name "Cain." So Eve is explaining why she gave her first born that name. But more importantly, I think, is the fact that Eve recognizes that the Lord was the ultimate source of this gift of a child. That says a great deal about Eve's spiritual outlook on life, even life outside the garden. She is definitely someone who regards God as being very much a part of her life.

Eve is certainly someone we could choose as a model of faith. And we learn all this from just the one line she spoke in the Bible!

†

In the Hebrew Bible the prophets are found in the middle of the book. But in Christian Bibles the prophets are found at the end of the Old Testament because so many of their oracles are fulfilled in Jesus Christ.

ZECHARIAH

Let's move on to another naming scene in the Bible, this one from the New Testament. Luke records for us the naming of the son of Zechariah and Elizabeth. All the relatives want to name the boy after someone in the family. But both Zechariah and Elizabeth know what the angel said his name should be. And so Zechariah writes plainly on the tablet presented to him, "His name is John" (Luke 1:63). Again, this is a short line. But it speaks volumes about the spiritual growth that has taken place within John's father. Recall that Zechariah had doubted the angel's words to him at first. That is the reason why he cannot speak. But over the course of nine months Zechariah has had plenty of time to think. And so when he writes those words on the tablet he is making a great statement of faith. He is saying that he now believes the angel and wants to give his son the name the angel said he should have. So Zechariah also serves as a model of faith for us because he learned to be an instrument of God.

JOB

Sometimes the biblical author will help us out by giving us some clues to help us interpret what we hear people say in the Bible. How often do we get that kind of help in everyday life?

A good example of this can be found in the first two chapters of the Book of Job. You may be thinking, Didn't we use Job as an example in Chapter 3 about focusing on people? Yes, we did. But Job is such a rich book, I just can't resist coming back to it for more.

The author tells us right away that Job is a great guy. We even hear the same from God. And when Job responds to the first set of tragedies in his life, we have to agree with everything we have been told about him so far. Job says,

†

"Naked I came from my mother's womb, and naked shall I return there; the LORD gave, and the LORD has taken away; blessed be the name of the LORD." (Job 1:21, NRSV)

The books of the Bible were not collected into a single bound volume by copyists until the fourth century, when the Christian Church was no longer persecuted in the Empire. Before that time the Scriptures existed as a collection of separate smaller books.

How many of us could make such a response in the face of such loss? It shows the high quality of Job's character.

But listen to what Job says at the end of the second set of tragedies:

"Shall we receive the good at the hand of God, and not receive the bad?" (Job 2:10, NRSV)

Does this sound the same as Job's first response? At first hearing it does. But on further reflection we might notice that Job asks a question here. He does not make a statement about God's ways as he did the first time. Now he labels things as good and bad. And note also that Job does not have a blessing for God this second time. This is where the author steps in to help us out a little. He tells us:

In all this Job did not sin with his lips. (Job 2:10, NRSV)

This makes us wonder what may be going on in his heart, especially since Job himself was very interested in what was going on in the hearts of his seven sons. As it turns out, the rest of the story is about what is going on deep down inside of Job.

JOSEPH

We all know about his coat of many colors, or as one Broadway musical had it, his "amazing technicolor dreamcoat." But, after a few years in Egypt, Joseph's dreams had less and less to do with the Promised Land. We know this because of what he says when he names his two sons. You will find the text at Genesis 41:50–52.

> Before the years of famine came, Joseph had two sons,
> whom Asenath daughter of Potiphera, priest of On,
> bore to him. Joseph named the firstborn Manasseh,
> "For," he said, "God has made me forget all my
> hardship and all my father's house." The second he
> named Ephraim, "For God has made me fruitful in the
> land of my misfortunes." (NRSV)

The footnotes in your Bible will probably help you make the connection between the name of each son and the reason Joseph gives for each name. To make a not-so-long story even shorter, Manasseh sounds like the Hebrew word for "forget" and Ephraim sounds like the Hebrew word for "being fruitful."

The bottom line is that Joseph clearly regards Egypt as his new home. He has a wife, a family and a good job. In fact, he is pretty much the CEO of all Egypt. Only the Pharaoh of Egypt ranks higher than Joseph. As long as Joseph keeps food coming to the pharaoh's table all is well.

In any other book, this might be the end of the story. It definitely has a they-lived-happily-ever-after kind of tone to it. But this is the Bible, and any story that ends with God's favorites in the land of Egypt is certainly not over yet.

How does Joseph get refocused on the Promised Land? This is where his father Jacob comes in for the rescue. The old patriarch gets to see his son again. But before he dies Jacob makes sure Joseph understands that the Promised Land is his true home. And sure enough, when Joseph is on his deathbed he has this to say to his assembled brothers:

> "I am about to die; but God will surely come to you,
> and bring you up out of this land to the land that he
> swore to Abraham, to Isaac, and to Jacob." So Joseph

made the Israelites swear, saying, "When God comes to
you, you shall carry up my bones from here." And
Joseph died, being one hundred ten years old; he was
embalmed and placed in a coffin in Egypt. (Genesis
50:24–26, NRSV)

Amazing isn't it? The same Joseph who was so sure Egypt was his new
home now makes his brothers swear to carry him to his real home
after he is dead. And the book concludes with the body of Joseph all
ready for transport to the Promised Land.

Once again, this striking faith journey is carried forward not so
much by narrative but by the words that come from the mouth of a
character.

Joseph's story gives us an example of another major feature in biblical accounts: dialogue. We heard Joseph speaking to his brothers
about just how important the Promised Land is for him and for them.
And in fact, when two people are talking in the Bible it is often the case
that one of them is more attuned to God than the other. Noting the
difference helps us learn a little more about the journey of faith. Let's
consider a few more examples.

JACOB AND PHARAOH

One of my favorite scenes in the Bible is the one where Jacob has an
audience with the king of Egypt. It was all arranged by Jacob's son,
Joseph. Imagine the imperial court, filled with evidence of Egypt's
great wealth. Then imagine the patriarch entering that court with all
his 130 years of life, the very thing the Pharaoh could not rival even
with all his resources.

Pharaoh might have asked Jacob any number of questions. He
might have asked him what it was like to raise a fine son like Joseph.
Or he might have asked him what he thought of the great empire of
Egypt. But he asks about the one thing even Pharaoh had to marvel at:
Jacob's great age. Long life was something Egypt was especially inter-
ested in. We know that they had a real fascination with the afterlife.

Standing before Pharaoh is someone who, from his viewpoint,
seemed to have the secret to longevity. Is Jacob far older than anyone
the king of Egypt had ever seen? Or does Jacob look too young to be
the father of twelve sons?

In any case Pharaoh's question reminds us readers that Jacob is someone close to the God of life. So the scene makes a contribution to one of the basic themes of the Bible: God is the source of life. Jacob, in fact, regards his own long life as meager in comparison to the longevity of his father and grandfather.

Unfortunately the king of Egypt seems to tire of the discussion prematurely. If only he had asked Jacob about the God of their fathers. But Pharaoh has no interest in anything beyond the reaches of his vast empire.

PETER AND SIMON THE MAGICIAN

In Acts 8:9–24 we read about an encounter between Peter the apostle and a man named Simon who thinks he can buy the kind of healing power displayed by the apostles. The conversation goes like this in the New Living Translation:

> "Let me have this power, too," he exclaimed, "so that when I lay my hands on people, they will receive the Holy Spirit!"
>
> But Peter replied, "May your money perish with you for thinking God's gift can be bought!"

Two worlds meet here. The magician supposes he is speaking to a fellow colleague with nothing more than a new technique for doing what he does. Peter, on the other hand, understands that technique has absolutely nothing to do with what he does because it is all a gift from God. To his credit, Simon the magician realizes his mistake immediately and asks Peter to pray for him.

This passage, as you might have guessed, provides the basis for the word "simony" or making a profit from spiritual works. We may be tempted to judge Simon harshly for his misguided understanding of things. But maybe we should reserve judgment. After all, have we ever thought we could barter with God? It would be it far more noble to trust in God's plan as we announce every time we say the Lord's Prayer, "Thy will be done."

JOHN THE BAPTIST AND HIS EXAMINERS

In the first chapter of John, certain priests and Levites approach the Baptist. They are on a mission. They have been sent by the religious authorities of the day to find out who this man is. They need an answer to take back to their superiors. We will follow this dialogue as it appears in the NRSV (John 1:19–37).

Instead of telling them who he is, John begins telling them who he is not! Most of us would find this kind of response less than satisfactory. But John has a purpose.

Remember his mission from God—he is to give testimony to the light. John came to tell people who Jesus is. He knows these examiners will never ask the right question. So he gives them a little help: "I am not the Messiah." Their follow-up question should be, "Who is this Messiah you are talking about?" That would give John the opening he needs.

The examiners miss the point altogether. They are too focused on John to be sidetracked. Their questioning becomes more pointed. "Are you Elijah?" John's answer is a terse "I am not." They press on, "Are you the prophet?" This time John gives them a dismissive single-word answer, "No."

The examiners seem exasperated. "Who are you? Let us have an answer for those who sent us. What do you say about yourself?"

This gives John another opportunity to steer them in the right direction. "I am the voice of one crying out in the wilderness, 'Make straight the way of the Lord,' as the prophet Isaiah said." Once again the Baptist ushers them towards the path that lead to Jesus. All they have to do is ask something like, "What is the way of the Lord?"

But the examiners will not take their focus off John. Unable to get John to talk about himself, they shift the questioning to what he does, "Why then are you baptizing if you are neither the Messiah, nor Elijah, nor the prophet?" Now we get a better idea about their interest in John. They want to know what authorizes him to go around baptizing people in the Jordan River.

John tries once more to draw their attention to the Lord. "I baptize with water. Among you stands one whom you do not know, the one who is coming after me; I am not worthy to untie the thong of his sandal." There it is! Another chance to ask the right question, something like "Who are you talking about?"

But the scene ends here. We can almost see the examiners shrugging their shoulders and just walking away. All the evangelist can say is, "This took place in Bethany across the Jordan where John was baptizing." We might even wonder if this somehow echoes the report the examiners brought back to their superiors: Subject questioned. No significant data to report. Recorded at Bethany across the Jordan.

The Baptist must have shaken his head in disbelief as he watched them walk away. Maybe he thought something like, "I can't believe they didn't pick up on a single hint I gave them." Of course, John's own disciples were a little slow on the uptake, too. We are told that the next day John gave more testimony about Jesus but got no response. The day after that John gives more testimony in the company of two disciples. At last we read, "The two disciples heard him say this, and they followed Jesus."

John certainly gave it his all. He continued to testify about Jesus until someone finally picked up on what he was saying. The whole scene recorded in the fourth gospel gives us a wonderful example of the potential for spiritual insights available in the recorded dialogues of the Bible.

At this point I hope you feel ready to explore some of the dialogues in the Bible on your own. A good starting place might be the dialogue between the parents of John the Baptist and their relatives recorded in Luke 1:57–66. You might also begin with the exchange between the blind man and the authorities in John 9. Or you might try some of my favorite dialogues from the Old Testament: Job and his wife (Job 1:9–10); Joseph and his brothers (Genesis 45); Abigail and David (1 Samuel 25:23–35); or Caleb and the people of Israel (Numbers 13:30–14:10).

Some helpful hints:
　　† Does the character sound like someone who trusts in God?
　　† What do you think the character values the most?
　　† Which character in a conversation seems closer to God?
　　† If God is speaking in a passage, check to see if anyone seems to
　　　be listening.

PRAYING WITH THE BIBLE

In Matthew 21:28–32 you will find the wonderful parable of the two sons. One son said he would do what his father asked of him but in fact never did. The other refused at first but then repented and carried out his father's wishes. As you read through this parable apply it to yourself. Imagine God asking you to be a faithful son or daughter. How would you respond?

In Numbers 13:30–33 Caleb, a true Israelite hero and a believer, tries to convince his fellow Israelites that God has the power to give them the Promised Land. But they refuse to listen to him because they have such a low estimation of themselves. As they say, "to ourselves we seemed like grasshoppers..." (Numbers 13:33, NRSV). The problem, of course, lies in their own lack of faith in God.

Use this passage as a focus for your own prayer. Ask God to give you the kind of faith Caleb had, the kind of faith that gives you the power to face difficulties and move forward in your life.

FOR REFLECTION

Ask the group to listen to a reading of Psalm 139. At the end of the reading ask them to discuss the kind of person they thought of as they were listening. You might begin by asking such questions as, Did they imagine someone old or young? Someone peaceful or troubled? The goal of this activity is to make the psalm real for them so they can more readily connect it with their own lives.

Choose someone to read aloud the dialogue between Tobit and his wife in Tobit 2:11–14. Then invite them to discuss which one of the two seemed to be closer to God. Do the same thing with the conversation between Jehosaphat and Ahab in 1 Kings 22:5–8.

CHAPTER SIX: CONVERSATIONS WITH GOD

So far we have explored the valuable spiritual insights that can come from just thinking about what human characters in the Bible say. It gets even more fascinating when we explore exchanges between people and God that are recorded in the Bible. Generally in such exchanges God is seeking to awaken a person spiritually. And, of course, since we are fortunate enough to "eavesdrop" on the conversation, there is an opportunity for us to be awakened spiritually, too. After all, God is not likely to be involved in idle chit-chat.

The Bible is the word of God. Whether God is presented in the Bible as actually saying anything or not, God is always addressing us as we read it. Every word in the Bible contributes in some way to the theme of salvation. This is true of the words placed in the mouths of human characters; it is especially true of words presented in the Bible as spoken directly by God. When a biblical passage presents God as speaking, we should listen carefully. It is like hearing the purest recording of a beautiful symphony with absolutely no static or interference of any kind.

Think about the first words from God in the Bible: "Let there be light." Have you ever thought about how appropriate it is that light is the first thing of which God speaks? Light is something so familiar yet also mysterious. There is likewise a benevolent quality about it. We can think of it as something outside of us, or as something within us. How appropriate that God speaks first of light. Just thinking about it can take us in a lot of directions rich with spiritual insight and discovery. In a sense, every word of God is like light, shining brightly, guiding us toward salvation and inviting us to faith.

Let's consider some conversations with God in the Bible and listen for the invitation to faith.

DIALOGUE BETWEEN GOD AND CAIN

In Genesis 4:9 we have an exchange between God and Cain after the murder of his brother Abel. I have chosen the reading from the New Living Translation because of its conversational tone.

> Afterward the Lord asked Cain, "Where is your brother? Where is Abel?"
> "I don't know!" Cain retorted. "Am I supposed to keep track of him wherever he goes?"

†

The word Bible comes from the name Byblos, *an ancient port north of modern-day Beirut. So much writing material came through this port that that Byblos became synonymous with things written. Thus, Byblos became associated with the sacred Scriptures.*

If Cain really listened carefully to what God says to him, he might hear in God's words an invitation to recognize the terrible thing he has done and ask God for forgiveness.

But Cain is not listening. In fact, he seems to dismiss any connection with Abel or with God. Instead of expressing remorse, he complains that God is punishing him too harshly and is even putting his life in jeopardy. In response to that, God will put a mark on Cain to protect him. But Cain still does not get the message and ends up just walking away from God's presence instead of drawing closer to God.

How do we picture Cain as he has this conversation with God? Is he shrugging his shoulders as if he could not care less? Is he still holding the club or the rock in his hand?

The text does not give us such graphic details. But I find it very helpful to picture the scene as vividly as I can to give it greater impact. The more clearly I can imagine a scene in my mind the more meaningful it becomes. For example, I might begin wondering about my own attitude in prayer.

Am I dismissive sometimes, acting as if it really doesn't matter what I do? Do I imagine, as Cain seems to have done, that God really does not care how I treat others? Sometimes, when I compare my own thoughts to the thoughts of Cain, he seems to be merely a distant relative. But at other times Cain can appear to be next of kin.

DIALOGUE BETWEEN GOD AND ISRAEL

Now let's consider a happier exchange. This is one of my favorites. It comes from the closing chapters of the Book of Isaiah. The Book of Isaiah begins with God searching for children who drifted away from God in spite of everything God did for them. But near the end of the book those children return. Listen to what they have to say to God:

Look down from heaven and see, from your holy and glorious habitation. Where are your zeal and your might? The yearning of your heart and your com-passion? They are withheld from me. For you are our father, though Abraham does not know us and Israel does not acknowledge us; you, O LORD, are our father; our Redeemer from of old is your name. (Isaiah 63:15–16, NRSV).

†

Our word paper comes from the Greek word papyrus. *Papyrus was a writing surface produced from the dried inner tissue of a reed common to the marshes of the Nile delta. Many ancient copies of the Bible were written on papyrus.*

Amazing, isn't it? At long last these children finally address God as "our father." Imagine how wonderful that must have sounded to God's ears! Of course, since it took them so long to come to this moment in their faith journey, the people are concerned that God may have forgotten about them. They ask God to look down from the divine dwelling place and take note of them. But God has not forgotten them at all. Listen to God's response to their plea for attention:

> I was ready to be sought out by those who did not ask,
> to be found by those who did not seek me. I said,
> "Here I am, here I am," to a nation that did not call on
> my name. I held out my hands all day long to a
> rebellious people… (Isaiah 65:1–2, NRSV)

God did not forget them at all. They were the ones who walked away and refused to listen to God's constant plea for them to come home. Doesn't this sound familiar? Doesn't it sound a lot like the parable of the Prodigal Son in Luke 15?

This dialogue makes us realize just how much God loves and cares for us. We may wander off to chase our dreams, but God is always there waiting to welcome us home again.

DIALOGUE BETWEEN JESUS AND NICODEMUS

Now let's look at the well-known dialogue between Jesus and Nicodemus in John 3:3–4. This time I follow the New Living Translation because I like the way it makes the conversation flow so naturally:

> Jesus replied, "I assure you, unless you are born again,
> you can never see the Kingdom of God."
> "What do you mean?" exclaimed Nicodemus.
> "How can an old man go back into his mother's womb
> and be born again?"

What makes this exchange so interesting is that Jesus and Nicodemus are speaking on two different levels. Jesus, of course, is trying to lift the conversation to a spiritual level. But Nicodemus takes his meaning on purely earthly grounds. Enjoying the near miss in his reply gives us the feeling of having an advantage over Nicodemus. And John the evangelist probably intended us to relish that advantage because the more aware of it we become, the keener we become at appreciating the spiritual level of so much in our own lives.

Actually this sort of thing happens a lot in John's Gospel. Jesus is constantly inviting the men and women he meets to ratchet their thinking up a notch or two so that they can move away from earthly viewpoints and become more familiar with spiritual ones. Consider, for example, our Lord's conversation with those around him about the bread of life. Or his conversation with the Samaritan woman about a well of life-giving water. I like to imagine that John's community relished such scenes when he told them about Jesus. They waited excitedly to hear what sort of response the Lord would receive from people when he spoke to them about himself and his mission.

DIALOGUE BETWEEN JESUS AND A BLIND MAN

Mark's Gospel records this exchange between Jesus and Bartimaeus, a blind man who has come forward to be healed:

> Then Jesus said to him, "What do you want me to do for you?" The blind man said to him, "My teacher, let me see again." (Mark 10:51, NRSV)

I've always found it curious that Jesus even asks this question. It must be obvious that Bartimaeus cannot see. Or does Jesus do this because he wants the rest of the crowd to hear the man's request? After all, the ability to really "see" is something everyone else could ask of Jesus, too. They can see physically, but they need to see spiritually. At least Bartimaeus knows what he needs.

Once again, picturing the scene as vividly as we can helps make it more meaningful for our reflection. How many people are standing around? Does Jesus look at them as he speaks to Bartimaeus? What do we see in the face of Bartimaeus as he pleads for sight?

This brief dialogue between Jesus and a blind man awakens some thoughts within me. Am I unable to see the things I need to see in my life? Am I blind to the spiritual treasures in life? Do I ever think to ask the Lord for help? Am I intimidated by those around me? Am I afraid to pray before a meal in a restaurant? Am I reluctant to speak up to protect another when everyone else is tearing him or her down?

KING SOLOMON'S PRAYER TO GOD

King Solomon was famous for his wisdom. Everyone is familiar with that wonderful dream of his in which he asks God for the guidance and insight to rule his people. God is so pleased that God not only grants this request but gives Solomon many other things besides.

But King Solomon seems to have lost his enthusiasm for God later in life. The biblical narrator tells us sadly:

> Then the LORD was angry with Solomon, because his
> heart had turned away from the LORD, the God of
> Israel, who had appeared to him twice, and had
> commanded him concerning this matter, that he should
> not follow other gods; but he did not observe what the
> LORD commanded. (1 Kings 11:9–10, NRSV)

And so Solomon's kingdom goes downhill. In fact, when he dies the kingdom breaks apart.

But Solomon makes a comeback, a second appearance in the Bible. And this time he is walking tall as a man of faith. We find him so in the Book of the Wisdom of Solomon.

This time Solomon does not just dream about praying for wisdom but makes a real deliberate prayer to God. We find his prayer in chapter 9. Here is a portion of it:

> ...give me the wisdom that sits by your
> throne,
> and do not reject me from among
> your servants.
> For I am your servant.... (Wisdom 9:4–5, NRSV)

This is biblical prayer at its best. Solomon not only asks for wisdom, but declares that he wants to serve God. And, of course, service to God is the ideal for any of us because we are created in God's image and likeness.

Now let's take a look at a passage from the Book of Wisdom where Solomon speaks about the way God governs the world. It reveals a lot about God's ways and how different they are from the ways of man.

> You spare all things, for they are
> yours, O Lord, you who love
> the living.
> For your immortal spirit is in all things.
> Therefore you correct little by little
> those who trespass,

> and you remind and warn them
>> of the things through
>> which they sin,
> so that they may be freed from
>> wickedness and put their trust
>> in you, O Lord. (Wisdom 11:26–12:2, NRSV)

The new Solomon certainly displays deep wisdom here. He recognizes that God's motivation is love for humanity. It sounds a lot like that famous line from the fourth gospel "For God so loved the world…" (John 3:16, NRSV). In fact, Solomon seems to have come up with a new phrase here: "you who love the living." All this is expressed with one word in the Greek language of the book (*philopsyche*), and it seems to be a word Solomon coined just for the occasion.

Another striking thing in Solomon's words to God here is his insight that God corrects people "little by little." Solomon pictures God here as patiently working with us, allowing us to learn from our mistakes so that in time we will draw closer and closer to God. Personally, I'm glad Solomon made his comeback. He gives us real wisdom here.

Are you ready to listen in on other conversations with God in the Bible? You may have some favorite passages of your own in mind already. If not, the Gospel of John is a good place to start since he offers a number of fascinating dialogues between Jesus and others. One example is his exchange with the woman of Samaria at John 4:7–26. She came to draw water and found the source of life. Another fine example is the very brief but moving dialogue between Jesus and the woman caught in adultery (John 8:9–11). If you are feeling especially energetic, you might enjoy the lively exchange between Jesus and some of the Pharisees in John 8:12–58.

Some helpful hints as you strike out on your own:
   † Pay special attention to words spoken by God the Father or Jesus the Lord.
   † Listen for the invitation to life in God's words.
   † Note the kind of response people give to what God says to them.
   † If they accept God's word, what advantages do they enjoy?

† If they do not accept God's word, what do they miss out on?

† For what reason would someone choose not to listen to God?

PRAYING WITH THE BIBLE

Psalm 73 begins this way:

> Truly God is good to the upright, to those who are pure
> in heart. But as for me, my feet had almost stumbled;
> my steps had nearly slipped. (NRSV)

This is a psalm about someone who really struggled to become a person of faith. The success of people who seemed to ignore God appeared for a while like an insurmountable obstacle to faith. But through prayer, the psalmist eventually recognized that such success was limited and that true success comes only with a right relationship with God.

As you read this psalm, insert a problem of your own into it and allow the grace of God to lead you to new insight.

FOR REFLECTION

Read aloud the dialogue between Abraham and God in Genesis 18:22–33. Have the group discuss the following questions: What do they think moves the patriarch to speak to God in this way? What does the conversation reveal about the way Abraham thinks of God and the way God thinks of Abraham?

CHAPTER SEVEN: GETTING THE PICTURE

When I am reading a passage of the Bible with a group of people, I like to ask them what they would do if they were to make a movie of it. What kind of location would they use? What sort of props would they need? Who would they choose to play the various roles in the scene? What would they have the actors wear? What kind of lighting would they choose?

My purpose in asking such questions is to get them to think about the biblical passage as vividly as they can. I believe that people can get much more out of a scene if they can clearly imagine it in their heads. It is not a matter of being absolutely right about such details, but getting them to really engage with the passage.

Allow me to offer an example. If I were to ask a group to choose someone to play the role of Moses, I'm almost sure most of them—from my generation, at least—would immediately announce Charlton Heston! That's an easy one because we have all seen Mr. Heston in that role and so it becomes an easy fit. But sometimes it is not so easy. I once asked a group what actress they would choose to play the role of the woman from Shunem in 2 Kings 4, a woman the author describes as "great," spiritually speaking, of course. That proved to be very challenging because each actress whose name came up had some qualities that recommended her and some that did not. In any case, the purpose is not to arrive at a consensus but just to get people thinking concretely about a character from the Bible. I am always surprised at the insights that surface in such discussions.

Let's look at a few examples and try to picture them as vividly as we can.

THE CANAANITE WOMAN

This well-known account comes from Matthew 15:21–28. We all marvel at the faith of this woman and her determination. Even in the face of apparent rebuffs from Jesus, she has the courage to persist with her pleas for Jesus to cure her ailing daughter.

Acting out this scene reveals a little detail that contributes a great deal to our admiration for this woman. If, in our reconstruction of the scene, we have all the disciples gathered around Jesus urging him to get rid of her, imagine what must take place next. In the New Living Bible we read:

> But the woman came and fell at his feet and cried, "Help me, sir."

How did this Canaanite woman get close enough to Jesus to fall at his feet and make her request? Did she push her way through the disciples to get that close? Did they step aside as she drew near, eyeing her with disdain as she passed in front of them?

Some books of the Bible have more than one name. Chronicles can also be called by its Greek name, Paralipomenon. *Sirach has a Latin name,* Ecclesiasticus. *And Ecclesiastes has a Hebrew name,* Qohelet.

The text is not detailed enough for us to reconstruct exactly what took place. But if we imagine the Canaanite refusing to allow the disciples to come between her and Jesus, it really makes this account come alive for us. And this woman becomes the true model of faith Jesus proclaims her to be at the end of the account.

The effort we put into a vivid portrayal of this scene from Matthew can lead us to deeper insights for ourselves. Would we ever allow anyone or anything to come between us and Jesus?

THE WEDDING AT CANA

This scene is familiar to everyone. We have all seen this one represented on canvas and perhaps even on the silver screen. Where do we imagine the wedding feast taking place? Is it outside under a canopy? Is it in a large courtyard with colorful banners hanging on the walls? How many guests are there? What are they wearing?

Acting out this scene will inevitably force you to ask this question: At precisely what point does the water became wine?

Almost everyone says it was when the waiters drew some water out of one of the six jars and took it over to the "master of ceremonies" (as he is called in the New Living Translation).

But consider another possibility. What if we think of the water becoming wine earlier in the account, when they drew it from the well or spring to fill the six jars. That might help explain why they filled the jars "to the brim." They wanted as much of this better wine as they could get, but at the same time they did not want to waste any of it by having it spill out of the jars.

Both insights are possible. John's account isn't so tightly woven as to rule out one or the other. But it is intriguing to explore the implications of each one.

The more customary explanation accents the moment of discovery, when the master of ceremonies tastes the water that had just then become wine. This might lead us to think about times in our own lives when we have had a similar moment of discovery, and perhaps have even been moved to tears by some sudden awareness of God's great love for us.

The second scenario accents the immeasurable character of God's grace. There is an unlimited supply of it. The only limitation is our capacity to make room for it in our lives.

Either response leads to deeper insights into our own relationship with God. And that is the reason for asking the question in the first place.

THE WALLS OF JERICHO

This is a familiar passage from the Book of Joshua and another one we have seen on canvas or the silver screen. We have all "seen" the walls come "tumbling down" as the songs says. There they lie in a heap all around the city. All the Israelites have to do walk over them and take the city.

But wait! Let's consider this question. How did Rahab and her whole family survive the collapse of the walls? We read in chapter 2:15 of Joshua that Rahab lived in the wall of the city. How did her family escape being crushed by the weight of the stones?

It seems to me there are at least two explanations: either God protected the woman and her family as the walls came down around them, or, the portion of wall in which she lived did not collapse at all but remained standing.

Once again, we will never know the answer to such a question. But the experience of trying to imagine the scene as vividly as we can helps us appreciate all the more the fact that God did protect this faithful woman and her family. And that discovery may lead us to appreciate the many wonderful gifts we take for granted each day.

WATERS OF LIFE

I remember getting really thirsty while traveling on the highway. Suddenly the only thing that mattered was finding a road sign announcing that a place to get a drink was just ahead. The highway became nothing more than a channel to get me to a drinking fountain.

Genesis 26 reminds me of that thirsty trip. It describes the way God used wells of water to lead Isaac back to the Promised Land.

Isaac is actually on his way to Egypt. But God appears to him and tells him specifically not to go there but remain where he is and God will bless him.

And God did just that. In time, Isaac becomes so prosperous the local residents (Philistines) invite him to leave. Since water is scarce in that territory, Isaac has to dig wells along the way. He gives each well a name. And if you take note of the names, it becomes a little like connecting the dots to make a picture. In other words, you see something you had not seen before.

> But when Isaac's servants dug in the valley and found
> there a well of spring water, the herders of Gerar
> quarreled with Isaac's herders, saying, "The water is
> ours." So he called the well Esek, because they

> contended with him. Then they dug another well, and
> they quarreled over that one also; so he called it Sitnah.
> He moved from there and dug another well, and they
> did not quarrel over it; so he called it Rehoboth, saying,
> "Now the LORD has made room for us, and we shall be
> fruitful in the land." (Genesis 26:19–22, NRSV)

Look at the names Isaac gives to those wells! Actually you need to look at the footnotes because they translate the names for you. Isaac calls the first well "Contention." He calls the second one "Enmity." And he calls the third one "Room." Do you see the pattern? Gradually God uses well of water to lead Isaac from oppression to freedom.

I find this to be a powerful image for my own life. When I look back on my life, I can identify certain people who benefited me the way a well of water benefits someone on a journey. I get the strong impression that God was leading me by these "wells of water" to bring me to this point in my life. And along the way it seems God was always leading me to a better place, just like God led Isaac to a better place.

You can give many passages of the Bible new life and color by imagining them as vividly as you can. How do you picture the scenery or the details? Or how do you picture the people involved? Their eyes? Their face? The way they move about? It might be best to start with a familiar passage from the Gospels. If you are looking for a starting place, you might begin with a miracle account such as the healing of the man with a withered hand (Mark 3:1–6) or the woman unable to walk upright (Luke 13:10–13).

Here are some leads to help you picture a biblical scene vividly.

    † Select a scene from the Bible.

    † Try to put a face on the characters, perhaps even coming up with a cast to play the various parts.

    † Think about details: background, color, lighting and actions.

    † Act out the scene in your mind or even in the room.

    † Did you notice anything you hadn't seen before?

    † Explore the implications each variation might have on your spiritual life.

PRAYING WITH THE BIBLE

The Babel account offers a fascinating study in human self-reliance. The people assume they can find complete security in a city with a tower, the product of their own hands. The ideal, of course, is that they should find security in God. So God makes it impossible for them to communicate with each other. They have to abandon their project. But now there is a chance for them to listen to God since they cannot listen to each other.

Think about the times you have contemplated building your own Babel, a time when you have looked for security in your own plans instead of in God. Pray that you will find the wisdom to listen to God

FOR REFLECTION

Select one of the scenes described in this chapter and have the group act it out. What do they notice as they do so? Did they discover things they did not know before? If you are looking for a place to start, begin with the account about the Canaanite woman.

Select an illustration of a biblical scene from a Bible or a book of art. Invite members of the group to study the illustration and then discuss it. What impression does the illustration make on them? Would they add anything to it? Where would they place themselves in the scene? You could do something similar with a scene from one of the videos listed among the helpful resources at the end of this book.

CHAPTER EIGHT: ENJOYING THE IMAGES OF THE BIBLE

Each one of us has been fascinated by a beautiful gemstone. Our first instinct is to pick it up and hold it to the light, turning it around and around. The slightest shift in angle when held against the light reveals a new depth of beauty.

It is much the same with the images of the Bible. We can think of each image as a gemstone, inviting us to pick it up in our mind and turn it this way and that. Each new angle brings new meaning and insight to light. This approach is especially applicable to the Psalms and the Prophets because of their fine poetic lines.

It may take some time getting used to using the images of the Bible this way. Be patient. There used to be special items in the newspaper featuring visual puzzles. If you stared at them long enough, a three-dimensional picture emerged from the surface of the paper and seemed to float in the air just in front of the page. A key piece of advice in the instructions read: Keep trying. It is that way with images in the Bible. Don't give up trying to see them in a new light. Keep trying.

THE LAMP

As an example, let's look at the image of the lamp in Psalm 119. The relevant verse is 105; this time I have chosen the text of the New

Living Translation because I prefer the more natural "for my feet" over the traditional "to my feet."

> Your word is a lamp for my feet
> and a light for my path.

What kind of lamp do we picture here? Do we think of a candle carried in the hand? Or do we imagine one of those clay lamps unearthed by archaeologists, shaped like a little gravy boat with a large looped handle? Or do we think of a light enclosed in a small metal canister with a handle, the door of the lamp swung open to let a beam of light escape? It might be helpful to actually draw the kind of light we imagine. That would give us something to look at as we meditate on this line.

Each way of thinking about the light brings with it new insights into the verse. If we think of the light as a candle, we might imagine it flickering in the wind. Maybe it is in danger of going out. Is our relationship with God like that sometimes? In danger of going out?

†

The earliest known physical evidence of a book from the New Testament is a fragment of papyrus discovered in Egypt in 1920. On it are preserved handwritten Greek verses from John 18. This manuscript is believed to date from the early part of the second century of our era.

If we think of the light as coming from one of those clay lamps pictured in archaeology books, it might lead us to consider the oil in the lamp. How much of it is there? Is there danger of it running out? The parable of the bridesmaids may come to mind (Matthew 25:1–13). Are we like the wise ones who were foresighted enough to bring extra oil? What efforts have we taken to ensure that the light of faith remains burning bright in our hearts?

Now let's think of the light as coming from a lantern carried by a handle, the kind of thing you might have seen in an antique shop. The lantern image introduces a new range of insights. The protective door to the lantern could suggest the security that comes to us from the word of God. The handle could suggest our attachment to the light. Do we have a sure hold on this lantern? Is there a chance we may drop it?

No matter what sort of lamp or lantern we have in mind, we could also ask what are we doing with the light. The rest of the Scripture talks about a path. Maybe we could think of the light as something we carry as we walk along a dark road. The light is needed to illuminate the road so we can see things we might trip over as we go along. Do we think of God's word that way? Guiding us through life, helping us avoid the things in life that might trip us on our spiritual journey?

THE BROKEN CISTERN

This Scripture passage is a favorite of mine. It must have been one of Jeremiah's favorites, too. The prophet refers to wells or cisterns several times in his book. The first time is in verse 2:13. The New Living Translation renders it this way:

> For my people have done two evil things: They have forsaken me—the fountain of living water. And they have dug for themselves cracked cisterns that can hold no water at all!

Cisterns are not a common sight anymore. When we need water we turn the tap and immediately (most of the time) get cold or hot water. But not too long ago people had to go to the cistern for water. I remember looking into one in the yard of our parish church. It had not held water for years. In fact, the groundskeeper was using the cistern as a place to pile grass clippings. As I stood above the opening to the cistern, I imagined what it must have been like in the old days to depend on such manmade holding tanks for something as precious as water.

It's precisely that manmade part that Jeremiah accents in the verse above. No matter how well-crafted, a cistern can have cracks in its walls. Once that happens the water begins to seep out of the tank. And just when you need it most, you will find the cistern dry. This makes the cistern a good image for representing the things people substitute

†

Hebrew manuscripts of the Bible more than a thousand years old are rare because copies of the Bible were carefully discarded, often buried in the ground, once they became worn, discolored, or otherwise damaged. This was done out of reverence for the sacred text.

for God in their lives. Their substitutes may prove useful for a while but ultimately they will fail us. Jeremiah would rather have his people turn to God who is a "fountain of living water," far superior to any manmade cistern.

What are the cisterns in our own lives? Those things we turn to for security and life instead of turning to God? Have we considered that these earthly resources may turn out to be just as unreliable as those cisterns were for the Israelites in the days of Jeremiah?

In chapter 38 of his book Jeremiah is actually thrown into a cistern belonging to a member of the royal family. The cistern had no water. All that remained was mud on the bottom. The chapter tells us "Jeremiah sank down into it." What a vivid description! It's fairly easy to imagine what the prophet experienced. Are our own spiritual cisterns filled with the waters of faith? Or are they running dry with nothing more than mud on the bottom?

THE THIRSTY DEER

The author of Psalm 42 uses a wonderful image to represent his longing for God. The first line runs this way in the New International Version:

As the deer pants for streams of water,
so my soul pants for you, O God.

Once again, as in the Book of Jeremiah, God is compared to streams of water. But this time our attention is drawn to the thirst for such streams. Why does a deer pant for such streams? Because it instinctively knows its life depends on it. That insight alone makes this a fitting image for our relationship with God.

But there is more to this image. The deer generally does not stray far from the streams; it grazes nearby, going back frequently for a drink. Shouldn't it be that way with us? We should never stray far from God but go back frequently to find refreshment. The deer follows the course of the stream. Likewise we should follow God, allowing the word of God to determine the course we take in life.

THE BURNING BUSH

Then Moses said, "I must turn aside and look at this great sight, and see why the bush is not burned up."
(Exodus 3:3, NRSV)

A bush engulfed in flames probably would not be the first choice for a modern version of Moses' encounter with God on the mountain. The fire part still seems state-of-the-art, but the bush is definitely passé. More likely, the special-effects technology of today would give us something like an elaborate throne dropping out of the sky.

We should not be too quick to dismiss the burning bush as an appropriate vehicle for a vision from God. Fire, of course, is standard imagery for the presence of the divine in the Bible. Think of the chariot of fire that appeared when the prophet Elijah went up into heaven, or the tongues of fire that appeared over the apostles on the day of Pentecost.

But what is the significance of a bush or a shrub? There is a defenseless character to it. It is certainly vulnerable to fire. In fact, flames would quickly consume it. Think of the words of Psalm 90 that compare mere mortals to the grass of the field that withers in the heat of the day.

And so the burning bush may be an appropriate image for the presence of the divine among the mortals of the earth. The fragile bush could be consumed by the fire. But by God's grace it is preserved. Mortals are equally fragile in the purifying presence of God, but God's love is so great that divinity and humanity can stand together. The account of the Exodus from Egypt explores over and over again this careful balance in the relationship between God and people.

INCENSE

Let's consider one more example. This one comes from another psalm. By this time it should be obvious that the Book of Psalms is a rich resource for powerful images that can nourish our faith.

> Let my prayer be counted as incense before you, and
> the lifting up of my hands as an evening sacrifice.
> (Psalm 141:2, NRSV)

At evening prayer services at Mount St. Mary's Seminary in Cincinnati, we sometimes have incense burning in the presence of the community as we sing this psalm. As we pray, the incense rises up to the chapel ceiling, visibly echoing the words of our prayer. The fragrance of the incense fills the chapel. And we ask that the prayers of the community be equally pleasing to God. It sometimes reminds me of the fragrance of Noah's sacrifice that was so pleasing to God when the world started all over again after the flood (Genesis 8:21).

As I reflect more about the incense, I have the insight that incense needs a fire to unlock its fragrance. And doesn't prayer need the fire of faith to make it pleasing to God? The fragrance of the incense can still be detected long after the smoke has dissipated. In the same way the "fragrance" of a prayer can still influence our day long after we have finished it and moved on to the more mundane things of life.

No wonder the psalmist wanted God to regard his prayer as incense!

If we turn these images over and over again in our minds, we could certainly come up with even more connections between them and our spiritual journeys. I have found it worthwhile to jot down insights that come to me as I ponder the images used by the biblical authors. I assume that the biblical authors have chosen just the right one to capture what they want to say. We have so much to gain by probing each image as much as we can to tease out all its richness.

I encourage you to try your hand at it. Select an image you have always found meaningful for you and hold it up to the light. Turn it this way and that. Let it reveal to you new insights into your own relationship with God.

Some helpful suggestions:
> † Read a line of biblical poetry slowly.
> † Try to imagine one image as vividly as possible. Perhaps even draw it.
> † In your mind try to look at it from many different angles.
> † How does each new angle help you appreciate your relationship with God?

PRAYING WITH THE BIBLE

In the course of his dialogue with his three friends, Job uses some striking images to express the loving attention God gave to creating him. Here is what Job says:

> Your hands fashioned and made me;
>> and now you turn and destroy me.

> Remember that you fashioned me like clay;
>> and will you turn me to dust again?
> Did you not pour me out like milk
>> and curdle me like cheese?
> You clothed me with skin and flesh,
>> and knit me together with bones and sinews.
> (Job 10:8–11, NRSV)

In the first image Job thinks of God as a potter, carefully shaping him like clay on a wheel. Then he thinks of God as a cheese maker, pouring him into a mold. Finally, he thinks of God as a tailor giving attention to every detail of his makeup.

FOR REFLECTION

What image would you choose to express the love and care God put into making you? Let the image become the focus of a prayer of thanksgiving to God.

What image best describes your prayer?

CHAPTER NINE: SALVATION IS THE KEY

A question I often hear at Bible presentations is, "Did this really happen?" I want to say immediately, "Yes," but then I'm confronted with the next logical question, "How do you know it happened?" and that is where I run into trouble. It is not easy to put together satisfactory proof for the events described in the Bible.

The Bible is a rich resource for historical data. Nelson Glueck, beloved former president of Hebrew Union College, had a passion for what some call "surface archaeology." Using the Bible as his roadmap, he found many of the places referred to in the Bible just by carefully looking for the imprint of human habitation on the hills and valleys of the Holy Land. But there are also many details in the Bible that cannot be proved using the tools of research. Could we ever prove, for example, precisely where along the Nile River the baby Moses was set afloat?

Such questions are often beyond our capacity to answer in a satisfactory way. But there is one question that can always be answered in a satisfactory way: "Why is this in the Bible?" And the answer is always, "Because it in some way contributes to salvation."

In their document on Divine Revelation (*Dei Verbum*), the bishops at the Second Vatican Council gave special attention to this salvific truth of the Bible. They encouraged us, when reading the Bible, to concentrate on the power of its message to lead us to God. Any other kind of truth (scientific, logical or historical) plays a subordinate role to this main purpose.

We can take a lesson from the Middle Ages. Artists were producing marvelously illustrated Bibles in those days. Their colorful illustrations would compare two scenes, one from the Bible, the other from everyday life. The reader would learn a rich spiritual lesson just by studying the two scenes together and reflecting on them. Such early picture Bibles trained the reader to concentrate on the saving truth of a biblical scene.

†

The Hebrew, Greek and English alphabets look very different today. But all three are related to an alphabet developed by the Phoenicians over three thousand years ago. A person familiar with our capital letters today would easily recognize some characters in the ancient Hebrew alphabet, notably A, M and O.

If you come to this chapter after reading any of the preceding chapters, you are already familiar with some techniques for finding the salvific truth in the Bible passages you read. The people, the spoken words, and the images of the Bible all contribute to this theme.

But a few more examples may be of help.

JOHN 4

I am always amazed by the way even the smallest details in a Gospel can help contribute to the theme of the passage. Consider the famous encounter between Jesus and the Samaritan woman at the well. As we might expect, Jesus awakens within her heart a deep desire for the word of life. As she runs back to the village to broadcast her discovery to everyone else, John adds this little detail: "The woman left her water jar..." (John 4:28, NAB). What might at first appear to be an oversight on her part becomes, upon reflection, a profound witness to the theme of the chapter. The woman has forgotten all about the physical water she came for because she has found a spiritual well of water in the words of Jesus.

LEVITICUS 13

That was fairly easy. Now let's consider a more challenging example. Let's look at Leviticus 13:1–2. It reads this way in the New Living Translation:

> The Lord said to Moses and Aaron, "If some of the people notice a swelling or a rash or a shiny patch on their skin that develops into a contagious skin disease, they must be brought to Aaron the priest or to one of his sons."

At first reading, this passage sounds like a feature from the popular *Grossology* exhibit about the human body. How could skin diseases possibly contribute in any way to our understanding of our relationship with God?

But think about it. The concern in this part of the law is protecting the people. Every precaution must be taken to limit the contact between those who are physically unclean and the rest of the community. Now let's shift the issue to the spiritual level. What if people were equally concerned about compromising the spiritual well-being of the community? We might recall what Jesus said about cleanliness: "It is what comes out of a person that defiles" (Mark 7:20, NRSV).

†

Saint Ambrose, bishop of Milan and mentor to Saint Augustine, called the Psalms a "gymnasium for the soul" because people could find in them inspiration to practice all the virtues. If he were writing today, Saint Ambrose might have called the Psalms "a spiritual fitness-center."

So passages like this one can be used effectively to alert us to deeper and more fundamental concerns touching on our relationship with God. And I think that is precisely why this material was included in Leviticus.

GENESIS 5

Let's consider one of those passages I regard as among the most challenging in the Bible—genealogies. I'm willing to bet most Bible readers pass over this material rather quickly. But taking some time with the passage does have its rewards.

We meet up with our first genealogy in Genesis 5. I must admit, at first sight it has a lot going against it. There are those unusual names. There are those unbelievably long lives. And there is a lot of repetition.

Did you notice an exception? There is no record that Enoch died! In 5:24 we are told that Enoch "was no more" because God took him. Now, of course, this could be just another way of saying he died. But then why not just say he died, especially in a list of so many others who died?

It seems that Enoch enjoyed a special favor from God. When he reached the end of his time on earth, God took him as God took Adam when he was first created and placed him in the garden. But why did Enoch gain such a wonderful gift? The answer seems to be that he "walked with God." So walking with God certainly has its reward.

What does it mean to walk with God? The answer to that question becomes more and more clear as we continue to read the Bible about others who did the same, others like Noah or like Abraham and Sarah. They learned to trust in God, even when it was difficult to do so. Noah was told to build a huge boat where there was as yet no water. Abraham and Sarah were told to expect a child when they were both past seventy.

So even a genealogy becomes a fascinating source of spiritual insight when the salvation theme is applied to it.

This salvation theme sheds some light on those long lives, too. We normally wonder, "How could they live so long?" But we might recall that Adam and Eve would have not died at all if they had never ignored God's protective word. So from that perspective we could rephrase the question and ask instead, "Why were their lives so short, since the very first couple was created to be immortal?"

Once again, from the faith perspective, passages like Genesis 5 take on a deeper meaning. They contribute to our appreciation of the benefits in store for those who give greater value to spiritual things than to material ones. The message of salvation is the key to finding the deepest meaning in a passage from the Bible.

I have enjoyed reading the Bible together with you in this book. I hope you feel that you now have in hand some tools you can use to make your own reading of the Bible more fruitful. Remember that the authors of the Bible are on your side, your spiritual side. They wrote the Bible under God's inspiration to guide you along your own faith journey. So always look for the spiritual message in their words.

Some helpful suggestions:

†	Always look for a spiritual message when reading a passage from the Bible.
†	Ask yourself, What am I learning about my relationship with God?
†	Don't overlook the details in a passage. They may serve as the key to open the door to its spiritual riches.

PRAYING WITH THE BIBLE

Visualize a wall in front of you. Describe what it looks like. For example, is it made of brick? Or stone? Now give the wall a name representing some difficulty in your life something that seems to get in the way of your relationship with God. Now ask yourself what biblical character you would choose to work with you in tearing down this wall. What tool would the two of you use to break it down?

Rework this experience into a prayer asking God for the gift of faith.

FOR REFLECTION

The genealogy of Jesus in Matthew chapter 1 is a real challenge to read aloud. Announce that you, the facilitator, are going to accept the challenge. Group members have probably heard it before, but ask them to listen as if hearing the genealogy for the first time. Ask them to imagine they are paging through a family picture album as they listen. You might even hand out a simple drawing of a family-tree (a trunk with branches) and invite them to fill it in as they listen with the names of the people they find most interesting. At the end of the reading, ask them to talk about what it was like for them to hear the genealogy this way.

Jesus invited his listeners to consider the lilies of the field. Invite someone to read aloud Matthew 6:28 or Luke 12:27. Invite the group to consider a lily and then discuss the insights gained from their reflection.

Complete the phrase "God of..." with the title of a book of the Bible or with the name of some biblical character. Ask the group to identify the image that comes to mind for each of them as they listen. Then discuss how the image contributes to their understanding of God's saving power. Some examples:

God of Exodus	worker of wonders
God of Isaiah	planter of vineyards
God of Elijah	God of whispers
God of Ezekiel	God of deep waters
God of Jacob	wrestling angel in the night

HELPFUL RESOURCES

Brown, Raymond E. *Responses to 101 Questions on the Bible*. New York: Paulist Press, 1990.

If you have a question about the Bible, this is the place to start looking for an answer. Fr. Brown offers brief and to-the-point responses to over 100 questions. In case you're curious about that 101st question, it's about the church in the New Testament. What makes this book especially helpful is that the questions are clustered together by subject matter. For example, all your questions about how to read the Bible can be found in one place.

Collegeville Bible Handbook, The. Collegeville, Minn: The Liturgical Press, 1997.

If you are looking for a friendly, easy-to-use guide to the Bible, this is it. Some of the finest scholars in the land produced a brief commentary on each book of the Bible. The reader is also treated to a host of pictures, maps and drawings that help make the text come alive. There is even a color-coded bar running across the top of each page to help the reader navigate through the many books of the Bible.

Deen, Edith. *All the Women of the Bible*. New York: Harper & Row, 1955.

Although this book has been around for a while, the Bible has not changed and the characters remain the same, so this book remains a valuable resource. Edith Deen includes something about every woman mentioned in the Bible, many of whom will no doubt be unfamiliar to you, at least until you read about them, and then you will find their stories priceless for spiritual insight. Over twenty years later Edith Deen published another book which is equally valuable: *Wisdom from Women in the Bible*. San Francisco: Harper & Row, 1978.

Mueller, Steve. *The Seeker's Guide to Reading the Bible: A Catholic View.* Chicago: Loyola Press, 1999.

This book approaches reading the Bible like getting ready to make a trip to a foreign country. Its three chapters offer many useful tips on getting ready and then actually beginning your journey through the Bible. It even offers a travel plan to guarantee that you will read through the entire Bible.

Paprocki, Joe. *God's Library: Introducing Catholics to the Bible*. Mystic, Conn.: Twenty-Third Publications, 2000.

The express purpose of this book is to help you get over your fear of reading the Bible. It draws on your knowledge of a library to help you understand the makeup of the Bible. There are lots of clever exercises, lists and even quizzes to help keep you interested as you read along.

Pilch, John J. *Choosing a Bible Translation*. Collegeville, Minn.: The Liturgical Press, 2000.

This brief twenty-four-page pamphlet offers a wealth of information and practical guidelines to help you choose just the right translation. In addition, Dr. Pilch provides the reader with a helpful overview of all the major English translations of the Bible.

Santa, Thomas M., C.SS.R. *The Essential Bible Handbook: A Guide for Catholics*. Liguori, Mo.: Liguori Publications, 2002.

This book gives you more than an introduction to the Bible. It also connects the Bible with the tradition of the Church. Its chapters include a generous supply of references to the Catechism of the Catholic Church. There is a chapter entitled "The Bible and the Sacraments" that includes scriptural passages associated with each one of the seven sacraments. There are also several chapters devoted to helping you pray with the Bible.

Scott, Macrina, O.S.F. *Bible Stories Revisited: Discover Your Story in the Old Testament.* Cincinnati, Ohio: St. Anthony Messenger Press, 1999.

The subtitle says it all. Sister Macrina offers you highlights from stories of many characters in the Bible and then follows up with a host of questions to help you connect their lives with your own.

Sloyan, Gerard S. *So You Mean to Read the Bible! Some Tips for Absolute Beginners.* Collegeville, Minn.: The Liturgical Press, 1992.

This short book—just sixty-eight pages—is loaded with helpful guidelines. For those of you led to believe that reading the Bible will shake your Catholic faith, Father Sloyan boldly declares, "Nothing in the Bible can threaten Catholic faith" (page 14). The chapter entitled "How to Read the Epistles of St. Paul" gives you a readable overview of the life and letters of the apostle to the Gentiles. Sloyan even offers tips on what not to look for when reading Paul.

Witherup, Ronald D. *The Bible Companion: A Handbook for Beginners.* New York: The Crossroad Publishing Company, 1998.

This book really does serve as a gentle companion to anyone getting started as a reader of the Bible. The author walks his readers through each book, discussing structure, content and interpretation. There are plenty of easy-to-read tables providing the vital statistics on each book. And each section ends with an exercise to help the reader apply the book to life.

Zyromski, Page McKean. *Pray the Bible.* Cincinnati: St. Anthony Messenger Press, 2000.

This user-friendly book offers you many insightful and practical ways to tap the deep wells of the Bible to give your prayer life new energy. I found Chapter Three: "Javelins and Other One-Liners" especially good for learning how to pray the Bible on those hectic days that seem to multiply spontaneously on our calendars.

INTERNET RESOURCES

I am only beginning to appreciate the richness available on the Web for information about the Bible. One day I simply entered the words "Catholic Bible guides" on the search line and came up with over thirty thousand sites to wade through. I certainly have not looked at all of them. But here are a couple I have found to be very helpful. And they are free! I have listed below just a few of the many resources useful to groups interested in informed discussion of the Bible.

www.nccbuscc.org/nab

This Web site comes to us courtesy of our Catholic bishops. It offers a lot of information. All you need to do is click on the topic you find interesting. One helpful feature is a calendar from which you can find the liturgical readings for any day of the month. You can also access any chapter of the Bible in the New American Bible translation.

www.biblegateway.com

This site will enable you to find any passage or single word in the Bible in a variety of translations. The only drawback is that none of the translations include our deuterocanonical books, such as Judith or Tobit.

www.Biblestudytools.net

This site offers you many resources on line to enrich your under-standing of the Bible. It also allows you to search for a biblical pas-sage by verse number or by content using nearly twenty English translations.

www.mustardseed.net

I found this site to be a lot of fun. It gives you a description of many characters in the Bible, focusing especially on their strengths/weaknesses and the spiritual lessons we can learn from these people.

www.AmericanCatholic.org

This is the Web site for St. Anthony Messenger Press. It will put you in touch with a rich variety of resources to help you get the most out of reading the word of God.

PRINT AND VIDEO RESOURCES

All of the following are available from St. Anthony Messenger Press, www.AmerianCatholic.org:

Journeys Into... series. Raymond Apicella takes readers on a journey through each of the three Synoptic Gospels. *Journeys Into Matthew* for example breaks the first Gospel into eighteen manageable lessons. The workbook approach is used to invite the reader to actively engage the text. Apicella uses a similar approach for Mark and Luke, also in the series. Carolyn Thomas, S.C.N., offers a breathtaking journey through John's Gospel.

The Vision of the Gospels. This is a series of four videocassettes, one for each gospel. Reverend Michael Himes makes connections between the faithful of the early days of the church and the faithful of today. The focus is on the challenge of discipleship. The videos can be purchased separately or as a unit.

DeSales Catholic Video Library. There are four complete series in this library. Each one is made up of eight one-hour videos that can be purchased separately or as a unit. Topics are: Basic Tools for Bible Study; The Old Testament Covenant; The Living Gospels; and The Writings of Paul. Each video offers two presentations filled with insights for understanding the Scriptures and praying with them.

Scripture From Scratch: A Basic Bible Study Program. Virginia Smith and Elizabeth McNamer offer a total of sixteen easy-to-listen-to one-hour presentations giving viewers an overview of the Bible. There are eight videocassettes, each one including two presentations. The videos can be purchased separately or as a unit.

Scripture From Scratch II: The World of the Bible. Another series of eight videotapes, also featuring Virginia Smith and Elizabeth McNamer. This series offers such topics as the geography of the Bible, the historical background, the religious culture and the person of Jesus. The videocassettes can be purchased separately or as a unit. There is also a study guide for the entire series.

PERIODICALS

Another valuable resource can be found in biblical publications coming out several times each year. They offer many valuable insights and by their nature are always timely and up-to-date. Here are some of my favorites:

Bible Review. This bimonthly magazine is published by the Biblical Archeology Society. It features very readable articles on the Hebrew Bible and the New Testament. A major plus is the wonderful illustrations and artwork in its pages, making the biblical text come alive for the reader. You can also order back issues in sets revolving around certain themes, such as the women of the Bible or art relating to the Bible. Web site: www.Biblereview.org.

The Bible Today. A very readable Catholic resource for over forty years, it is published six times a year by Liturgical Press. Each issue usually has a theme. The articles are generally brief and easy-to-read. Web site: www.litpress.org.

Scripture From Scratch. This is a monthly publication from St. Anthony Messenger Press. Each issue concentrates on one topic from the Bible, for example, the Biblical world or the meaning of suffering. Issues are four pages each, very readable and loaded with extras—questions for discussion, ideas for praying with the Bible, further reading. Web site: www.AmericanCatholic.org.

The Word Among Us. The purpose of this resource is best explained in their own words: "*The Word Among Us* is intended to assist people in reading, meditating on and understanding Scripture [and to] provide sound, practical advice for Catholics on the living out of the Christian life." Web site: www.wau.org.

SCRIPTURE INDEX

OLD TESTAMENT

NEW TESTAMENT